Today's Superst★rs

Entertainment

WITHDRAWN

Chris Rock

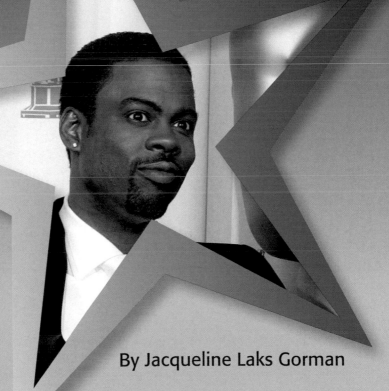

By Jacqueline Laks Gorman

 Gareth Stevens
Publishing

Please visit our web site at www.garethstevens.com.
For a free color catalog describing our list of high-quality books,
call 1-800-542-2595 (USA) or 1-800-387-3178 (Canada). Our fax: 1-877-542-2596

Library of Congress Cataloging-in-Publication Data
Gorman, Jacqueline Laks, 1955-
   Chris Rock / by Jacqueline Laks Gorman.
       p. cm. — (Today's superstars. Entertainment)
   Includes bibliographical references and index.
   ISBN-13: 978-0-8368-9235-2 (lib. bdg.)
   ISBN-10: 0-8368-9235-6 (lib. bdg.)
   1. Rock, Chris—Juvenile literature. 2. Comedians—United States—
   Biography—Juvenile literature. 3. Actors—United States—Biography—
   Juvenile literature. I. Title.
PN2287.R717G67   2008
792.702'8092—dc22 [B]   2008020730

This edition first published in 2009 by
Gareth Stevens Publishing
A Weekly Reader® Company
1 Reader's Digest Road
Pleasantville, NY 10570-7000 USA

Copyright © 2009 by Gareth Stevens, Inc.

Senior Managing Editor: Lisa M. Herrington
Senior Editor: Brian Fitzgerald
Creative Director: Lisa Donovan
Senior Designer: Keith Plechaty
Production Designer: Cynthia Malaran
Photo Researcher: Kim Babbitt

Photo credits: cover Ethan Miller/Getty Images; title page, p. 24: AFP/Getty
Images; pp. 5, 7 Frederick M. Brown/Getty Images; p. 9 Vinni Bucci/Getty
Images; p. 10 Kevin Mazur Archive 1/WireImage/Getty Images; p. 11 UPN/
courtesy Everett Collection; p. 12 Bettman/Corbis; p. 15 HBO/Photofest; p. 17
AP Images; p. 18 Warner Bros./courtesy Everett Collection; p. 20 AP Images;
p. 21 Scott Gries/Getty Images; p. 22 DreamWorks/courtesy Everett Collection;
p. 26 DreamWorks SKG/ZUMA/Corbis; p. 27 AP Images; p. 28 Frank Micelotta/
Getty Images.

Printed in the United States

1 2 3 4 5 6 7 8 9 10 09 08

Contents

Words in the glossary appear in **bold** type the first time they are used in the text.

Chapter 1 Sitcom Success

Chris Rock is at the top of the comedy world. His stand-up concerts always sell out. He has won awards for his comedy specials and for his late-night talk show. Rock has appeared in several hit movies. *Time* magazine even called him "the funniest man in America."

In fall 2005, Rock prepared for a new challenge. The TV series based on his life, called *Everybody Hates Chris*, was about to **premiere**. Like Rock, the main character was a poor African American kid who gets bused to an all-white school.

Rock's comedy had always been directed toward adults. *Everybody Hates Chris* was aimed at a much younger audience. Could Rock's humor translate to a family show?

Good Ratings, Glowing Reviews

Everybody Hates Chris first aired on September 22, 2005. Viewers definitely *did not* hate Chris. Nearly 8 million people tuned in to the first episode. The UPN network had its best rating ever for a **sitcom**. The show was a hit with **critics**, too. They called it "the best family sitcom on television" and "a laugh-out-loud show." They especially liked Tyler James Williams, who plays the character of Chris.

Rock had Tyler James Williams laughing during an interview to promote *Everybody Hates Chris.*

5

Kids Just Want to Be Chris

A lot of Chris Rock's humor is for adults only. But *Everybody Hates Chris* and his animated movies have made Rock popular with kids, too. In 2006, he received the Wannabe Award at the Kids' Choice Awards. Each year, the award is given to the star whom kids most "want to be." Other stars who have won the award include Will Smith, Adam Sandler, and Cameron Diaz.

Rock won another Kids' Choice Award that year. He was named the best voice in an animated movie for *Madagascar.*

Secrets to Success

Viewers of all ages related to the character of Chris. Like a lot of teens, he often feels as if the whole world is against him. He gets beaten up by bullies. He is blamed for things his sister did.

Rock doesn't appear on the show, but he is a big part of the program's success. He oversees and approves each script. He also **narrates** each episode. In that role, Rock delivers some of the funniest lines on the show.

After its strong start, *Everybody Hates Chris* lost viewers as the season went on. The show aired at the same time as popular shows on other networks. Still, it earned millions of loyal fans.

Fact File

Rock came up with the name *Everybody Hates Chris*. The show's title was a play on the name of the popular sitcom *Everybody Loves Raymond.*

Everybody Hates Chris also earned awards. In 2006, the show won the NAACP Image Award for outstanding comedy series. The Image Awards are given each year to people of color for their work in entertainment and literature. In 2007, Tyler James Williams won the award for best actor in a comedy series.

The third season of *Everybody Hates Chris* ended in May 2008. On the show, young Chris was more mature and confident. He also was starting to show his talent as a comedian. In a lot of ways, he was beginning to be more like the real Chris Rock.

Rock and the cast of *Everybody Hates Chris* celebrated their win at the 2006 NAACP Image Awards.

Chapter 2: Challenging Childhood

Christopher Julius Rock II was born on February 7, 1965, in Georgetown, South Carolina. He lived with his parents, Julius and Rose, in a nearby town called Andrews. Julius and Rose wanted to escape the **prejudice** they faced in the South. When Chris was 6, his family moved to New York to make a better life.

At first, they rented an apartment in Brooklyn. Soon, Chris's parents bought a house in a neighborhood called Bedford-Stuyvesant, or Bed-Stuy. Like Chris's family on *Everybody Hates Chris*, the real Rock family didn't have a lot of money. Chris's dad drove a newspaper delivery truck and worked other jobs. His mom taught mentally disabled children.

Fact File

As a child, Chris wanted to become a boxer, a comedian, or the president of the United States.

Trying to Be Better

Chris was the oldest of seven kids. He has five brothers and one sister. Their house was always crowded, especially since the family often took in **foster children**.

Julius and Rose were strict but loving parents. They taught their children the value of hard work. They also taught Chris and his siblings to be proud of themselves. In his book *Rock This!* Chris wrote that his mother "didn't teach us to believe we were as good as everybody else; she raised us to believe we were *better*."

In March 2003, Chris received a star on the Hollywood Walk of Fame. His mother joined him for the ceremony.

Bedford–Stuyvesant

Chris grew up on Decatur Street in Bedford-Stuyvesant. The tree-lined block was one of the nicest in the neighborhood. Yet Bed-Stuy is one of New York's toughest sections. When Chris was growing up, most people in Bed-Stuy were poor. The area had thousands of empty lots and buildings. Crime and drugs were major problems.

Many people from Bed-Stuy worked hard and made better lives for themselves. Chris wasn't the only one to make it big. Many hip-hop stars, such as Jay-Z, Mos Def, and Notorious B.I.G., came from Bed-Stuy.

Chris and Jay-Z grew up in the same neighborhood.

Fact File

Chris jokes that Bed-Stuy was so dangerous that no one would deliver pizza there. "My dreams weren't as grand as my life has become," he joked to *The New York Times*. "My dream was just to have food delivered to my house."

Getting on the Bus

Julius and Rose were worried about the schools in Bed-Stuy. They thought Chris would get a better education at a school in another neighborhood. Beginning in second grade, Chris went to school in a white neighborhood. Each day, he took a bus to the other side of Brooklyn. He was one of the few African American students in the school.

Early to Rise

Chris had to get up very early to catch the bus. Lack of sleep made it hard for him to focus in school. "I had to get up every morning at 6:00 A.M. to go to school to compete with white kids who didn't have to wake up until 8:00 A.M.," he wrote in *Rock This!* "That's not fair. One teacher said, 'Chris can't read.' I thought, 'No. Chris is ... tired.'"

Chris also faced a lot of **racism**. He was put into a special class for children who had learning problems. Chris didn't have trouble learning, however. He said the school just wanted to keep black students separate from white students.

On *Everybody Hates Chris*, the school bully constantly stuffs Chris in a locker. As narrator, Rock joked, "I started writing my first HBO special in a locker."

In the 1970s, African American students in many cities were bused to schools in white neighborhoods.

Busing to Better Schools

Through much of U.S. history, schools were **segregated**. African American kids and white kids went to different schools. The black schools often had old desks and out-of-date textbooks. In 1954, the U.S. Supreme Court ruled that segregated schools were against the law. Schools in many states were slow to change, however.

In the 1970s, many cities used a new plan to **integrate** schools. Black children in those cities were bused to schools in which most students were white. Many white people fought to keep black children out of those schools. Their protests sometimes turned violent. Although the law was on their side, the black children—including Chris—often faced prejudice at their new schools.

Difficult Days

When he got older, Chris was bused to Marine Park Junior High School and then James Madison High School. Both schools were mostly white. "It was also hard being the only black kid in my class," he later joked in his comedy act. "Whenever they would do that lesson on slavery, everyone would turn around and look at me!"

Chris got more than strange looks. He was called names, spat upon, and beaten up. "I was so outnumbered, so I would just stand there and take it," he told *Rolling Stone* magazine. "The worst part is that, after a while, your spirit is broken."

Chris dropped out of school when he was 17. He worked at Red Lobster and had other low-paying jobs. He wanted to do something bigger and better with his life.

The Importance of Education

Although Chris dropped out of school, he realizes the importance of education. He often says he would have trouble finding a good job today. "I have no real skills," he said in one interview. "If I picked up a paper right now and went through the want ads, there's nothing I could get that would pay more than the **minimum wage**."

Chapter 3

Making a Name in Comedy

Chris hated the jobs he had after leaving school. He had always been good at making people laugh. He loved to listen to comedians, such as Bill Cosby and Richard Pryor. Chris decided to follow in the footsteps of his idols.

Hitting the Comedy Clubs

In 1985, Chris went to an open-mike night at a comedy club called Catch a Rising Star. On open-mike night, anyone can go onstage and perform. Chris decided to tell some of his jokes. The crowd liked what they heard. Still, Chris was paid only $5. The pay wasn't good, but it was a start. Chris still had to work during the day. At night, he began performing at Catch a Rising Star and other comedy clubs.

Fact File

Chris isn't the only top comedian to get his start at Catch a Rising Star. Ray Romano, Jerry Seinfeld, and Robin Williams also began their careers at the club.

Getting a Big Break

Chris got his big break in 1986. One of his idols, Eddie Murphy, saw him performing at a club called the Comic Strip. Murphy liked Chris's routine. At the time, Murphy was one of the biggest stars in Hollywood. He got Chris a spot in an HBO special for new comedians called *Uptown Comedy Express.*

Murphy also helped Chris land his first movie role. He appeared with Murphy in the 1987 hit *Beverly Hills Cop II.* Chris was paid $600 for acting in just one scene.

Chris (bottom left) was one of five comedians who performed on *Uptown Comedy Express.*

15

Live From New York

In 1990, Chris tried out for the popular TV show *Saturday Night Live*, or *SNL*. He was asked to join the cast for the 1990–1991 season. For the first time, he was making a good salary doing what he loved.

Working on *SNL* was frustrating for Chris, however. He didn't like performing material written by other people. He also didn't appear in as many sketches as he wanted. He decided to leave the show after just three years.

Later, Chris admitted he had not worked hard enough to succeed on the show. He often stayed out late and missed rehearsals. His time on *SNL* was not all bad, though. He became close friends with other cast members, especially Adam Sandler and David Spade. "Those are my boys for life," he said. "I love those guys." Chris also learned a lot from being on *SNL*. "It's the absolute best training you can have in show business," he said.

Fact File

Chris had trouble managing the money he made on *Saturday Night Live*. He saved $50,000 in the bank and then spent $40,000 on a Corvette. After buying insurance for the car, Chris ended up $2,000 in debt!

Saturday Night Live

Saturday Night Live is the longest-running comedy series on TV. It has been on the air since October 1975. The 90-minute late-night show is performed live each week. *SNL* features comedy sketches starring the show's cast and a guest host. Many cast members create popular regular characters. One of Chris's favorite characters was an angry talk-show host named Nat X.

The *SNL* cast has changed many times over the years. Many cast members later became major stars, including Bill Murray, Eddie Murphy, and Will Ferrell. Mike Myers, Chris Farley, and Adam Sandler were the top stars during Chris's years on the show.

New Direction

During his time on *SNL*, Chris appeared in a few movies. In *New Jack City*, he showed that his talent wasn't limited to comedy. He earned excellent reviews for playing a drug addict in the film. In 1993, Chris had his first starring movie role. He played a rapper in the comedy *CB4*. Unfortunately, the film wasn't a hit.

Chris had hoped that *SNL* would help his acting career, but it didn't. When good acting parts did not come his way, he got serious about stand-up comedy.

In *New Jack City*, Chris played a drug addict. Ice-T (right) played a cop who tried to help him turn his life around.

Chapter 4 Breaking New Ground

In the mid-1990s, Chris appeared in a few movies and TV episodes. But he concentrated mainly on stand-up. He also had a new interest. He met a young woman named Malaak Compton at an awards show. She arranged special events for **UNICEF**. They soon began dating and were married on November 23, 1996.

Things were going well for Chris, but he was still not considered a major star. Everything changed in June 1996. That month, his second HBO special, *Bring the Pain*, became an instant hit. Audiences thought Chris was hysterical. Critics praised him for the honest, funny way he talked about real problems. Chris was hailed as the best young comedian in the business.

Bring the Awards!

Bring the Pain won two Emmys, the top awards for TV. Chris also released a comedy album called *Roll With the New*. It included the best routines from *Bring the Pain*. The album won a Grammy, the top award for music and other recordings.

Suddenly, Chris was hot. In 1997, he got his own talk show on HBO, *The Chris Rock Show*. Chris was the **executive producer** and one of the writers. The show featured hilarious sketches and interviews with famous guests. *The Chris Rock Show* won two Emmys before ending its run in 2000.

Chris was proud to show off the two Emmys he won for *Bring the Pain*.

Chris uses humor to make serious statements about the way people think and live.

Chris's Comedy

Chris has never been afraid to speak his mind—no matter whom he might offend. "For me, anything goes when I pick up a mike," he explained to *Rolling Stone*.

In his stand-up act, Chris tackles **controversial** subjects. He uses humor to make serious statements about the way people think and live. For example, he talks honestly about the issues of race and class in the United States. Chris uses a lot of bad language in his act. His comedy is definitely not for younger audiences. "I'm not trying to hurt people," he told *Rolling Stone*. "I look at myself as a reporter."

Bigger and Better

Offers to appear on TV shows and in films poured in. Chris hosted the MTV Video Music Awards in 1997 and 1999. His third HBO special, *Bigger & Blacker*, aired in July 1999. Chris won his second Grammy for the album from that show.

Chris also starred in a number of movies, including *Lethal Weapon 4* and *Down to Earth*. The 2003 film *Head of State* was an important one for Chris. He had already written and produced movies, but this film was his first as a **director**. In the movie, Chris plays a man who runs for president. In a way, he fulfilled his boyhood dream of becoming the president of the United States!

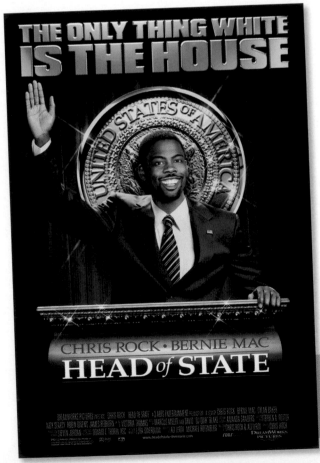

Head of State opened at number one at the box office in March 2003.

Chapter 5

No Apologies

Late in 2003, Chris took a break from film work and returned to comedy. He went on his first comedy tour in several years. His Black Ambition Tour traveled to 65 cities in the United States and Canada.

As usual, Chris talked about topics such as race and politics. For the first time, he also talked about being a father. A year earlier, on June 28, 2002, he and Malaak had their first daughter, Lola.

The Black Ambition Tour was a big success. One of the concerts became his fourth HBO special. That concert, called *Never Scared*, aired in April 2004. In the same month, Comedy Central ranked Chris number five on its list of the 100 Greatest Stand-Ups of All Time.

Hosting the Oscars

In 2004, Chris was asked to host the Academy Awards, or Oscars. They are the top awards for movies. It was a big honor for Chris. Millions of people watch the show. The host often gets more attention than the winners. The show's producers hoped Chris would attract younger viewers and make the show more up-to-date.

To prepare for the job, Chris watched the nominated movies and past Oscar shows. He also tried out new material at comedy clubs. During the show, Chris got a lot of laughs and kept his jokes clean.

Chris was the first African American man to host the Oscars since 1983. His idol Richard Pryor cohosted the show that year.

Tracing His Roots

In early 2008, Chris learned that he has an impressive ancestor. His great-great-grandfather, Julius Caesar Tingman, was a slave in South Carolina. After Tingman got his freedom, he fought for the North in the Civil War. After that, he served in the South Carolina state government. The news moved Chris to tears. "I'm very proud of my great-great-grandfather," he said.

Busy Year

Chris's schedule was crowded in 2005. Two of his films came out on the same day in May. He starred with his friend Adam Sandler in *The Longest Yard*. He also provided the voice of Marty the zebra in *Madagascar*. The animated hit was the first of his films that was suitable for his daughter to see. He also began working on his TV series *Everybody Hates Chris*.

Buzzing With the Best

Chris's work on *Everybody Hates Chris* kept him busy. He still managed to provide the voice of a mosquito in the 2007 animated film *Bee Movie*. The film was written by his good friend Jerry Seinfeld, who also voiced the main character. Chris is proud of the film. "I'm just happy to be in anything good and work with the best," he said. "Jerry Seinfeld is the best."

Fact File

In March 2005, *Never Scared* won a Grammy for best comedy album. It was the third time Chris had won the award.

Chris took a break from recording the voice of Marty in *Madagascar*.

Voice Acting

Chris is known for his unusual, high-pitched voice. It's no wonder that he has done voices for a lot of hilarious characters. In the mid-1990s, he was the voice of the puppet Lil Penny in popular commercials for Nike. In movies, he has played a guinea pig in *Doctor Dolittle* (1998) and a white blood cell in *Osmosis Jones* (2001). He also voiced Marty the zebra in *Madagascar* and Mooseblood the mosquito in *Bee Movie*.

Doing voice work is very different from regular acting. In a studio, actors stand in front of microphones to record their lines. They often record their lines alone, without the other actors in the film. That doesn't bother Chris. "I'm a comedian, so I'm used to working alone," he says.

Giving Back

Chris also finds time to give back to the community. He has appeared in many concerts and telethons to raise money for people in need. In 2007, Chris and Malaak arranged a holiday shopping trip for 175 low-income children in Brooklyn.

In late 2007, Chris kicked off a comedy tour called No Apologies. For the first time, he took his act to England. He also played sold-out shows across the United States and Canada. The name of the tour could well sum up Chris's career. He is proud of his success and doesn't feel that he has to apologize for any of it.

Fact File

In 2008, Malaak was one of the judges on the reality series *Oprah's Big Give*.

In 2007, Chris took part in a program with former President Bill Clinton (left). They joined Shakira, Bono, and other stars to inspire young people to get involved with social causes.

Family Man

Today, Chris's main concern is his family. He and Malaak had a second daughter, Zahra, on May 22, 2004. They live in the town of Alpine, New Jersey. Chris says that he tries to be a strict father and that bad language is not used in his house.

Chris says that having children has helped his career. "Everything I've done since I've had kids is better than the stuff I did before I had kids," he told *Life* magazine. They have given him more than good material. They have also made him happy. As he told Oprah Winfrey, "Taking care of my children is more fun than anything in the whole world."

Chris's whole family attended the 2006 Kids' Choice Awards.

Rock Keeps Rolling

What's next for Chris? He says he just wants to keep working on worthwhile projects. "You can't take for granted what it means to be involved in something good," he said. "So whenever I get the opportunity to work with good people, I really savor it and I thank my stars." Chris's fans know he will always be involved in good projects. He will always make them laugh.

Time Line

1965 Christopher Julius Rock II is born on February 7, in Georgetown, South Carolina.

1985 Performs his first stand-up routine, at Catch a Rising Star comedy club in New York City.

1987 Appears in the film *Beverly Hills Cop II* and on the HBO special *Uptown Comedy Express*.

1990 Joins the cast of *Saturday Night Live*.

1996 Stars in the groundbreaking HBO special *Bring the Pain*; marries Malaak Compton.

1997 Gets his own talk show, *The Chris Rock Show*; wins two Emmy Awards for *Bring the Pain*; writes the best-selling book *Rock This!*

2005 Hosts the Academy Awards; appears in the film *The Longest Yard* and provides the voice of Marty in *Madagascar*; creates the television series *Everybody Hates Chris*.

2007 Voices Mooseblood the mosquito in *Bee Movie*; launches the No Apologies comedy tour.

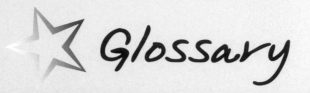# Glossary

controversial — leading to a lot of arguments

critics — in entertainment, people whose job is to give their opinions about movies, TV shows, or music

director — a person who is in charge during the filming of a movie or TV show

executive producer — a person who gets the money and organizes the people to make a movie or TV show

foster children — children who are cared for by other families, because their own families cannot care for them

integrate — to bring people together, regardless of race, color, or religion

minimum wage — the lowest rate of pay allowed by the law

narrates — tells the story of a TV show or movie, usually without appearing on-screen

prejudice — unfair treatment of people because of their race, color, or religion

premiere — to be shown in public for the first time

racism — hatred of people because of their race or skin color

segregated — separated based on race or skin color

sitcom — short for "situation comedy"; a TV comedy series that has the same characters each week

UNICEF — the United Nations Children's Fund; a part of the United Nations that helps children around the world

To Find Out More

Books
Everybody Hates School Dances. Everybody Hates Chris (series). Brian James (Simon Spotlight, 2007)

Movie Acting. Making Movies (series). Geoffrey M. Horn (Gareth Stevens, 2007)

DVDs
Bee Movie (DreamWorks Animation, 2008)

Everybody Hates Chris, Seasons 1, 2, and 3 (Paramount, 2006, 2007, and 2008)

Head of State (DreamWorks, 2003)*

The Longest Yard (Paramount, 2005)*

Madagascar (DreamWorks Animation, 2005)

* Rated PG-13

Web Site
www.thewb.com/shows/everybody-hates-chris
The official web site for *Everybody Hates Chris* has biographies of the cast members, video interviews, and full episodes of the show!

Publisher's note to educators and parents: Our editors have carefully reviewed this web site to ensure that it is suitable for children. Many web sites change frequently, however, and we cannot guarantee that a site's future contents will continue to meet our high standards of quality. Be advised that children should be closely supervised whenever they access the Internet.

Index

About the Author

Jacqueline Laks Gorman has been a writer and an editor for more than 25 years. She grew up in Brooklyn, New York, and attended the same junior high school and high school as Chris Rock—although in different years. She also attended Barnard College and Columbia University, where she received a master's degree in American history. She has written several series for children and young adults. She now lives in DeKalb, Illinois, with her husband, David, and children, Colin and Caitlin.

ISSUES THAT CONCERN YOU

Obesity

Lauri S. Scherer, *Book Editor*

GREENHAVEN PRESS

A part of Gale, Cengage Learning

GALE
CENGAGE Learning·

Detroit • New York • San Francisco • New Haven, Conn • Waterville, Maine • London

Elizabeth Des Chenes, *Director, Publishing Solutions*

For more information, contact:
Greenhaven Press
27500 Drake Rd.
Farmington Hills, MI 48331-3535
Or you can visit our Internet site at gale.cengage.com

For product information and technology assistance, contact us at

Gale Customer Support, 1-800-877-4253
For permission to use material from this text or product, submit all requests online at
www.cengage.com/permissions

Further permissions questions can be e-mailed to permissionrequest@cengage.com

Articles in Greenhaven Press anthologies are often edited for length to meet page requirements. In addition, original titles of these works are changed to clearly present the main thesis and to explicitly indicate the author's opinion. Every effort is made to ensure that Greenhaven Press accurately reflects the original intent of the authors. Every effort has been made to trace the owners of copyrighted material.

Cover image © Kokhanchikov/Shutterstock.com.

LIBRARY OF CONGRESS CATALOGING-IN-PUBLICATION DATA

Obesity / Lauri S. Scherer, book editor.
    pages cm. -- (Issues that concern you)
  Summary: "Issues That Concern You: Obesity: This series provides readers with information on topics of current interest. Focusing on important social issues, each anthology examines its subject in a variety of ways, from personal accounts to factual articles"-- Provided by publisher.
  Includes bibliographical references and index.
  ISBN 978-0-7377-6298-3 (hardback)
 1. Obesity--Juvenile literature. I. Scherer, Lauri S.
  RC628.O22 2013
  616.3'98--dc23
                                                            2012043706

Printed in the United States of America
1 2 3 4 5 6 7 17 16 15 14 13

CONTENTS

Firmly established as a hot-button issue of the twenty-first century, the problem of obesity has no easy solutions. There remains enormous debate over whether the government should play a role in reducing obesity, and if so, whether it should spearhead programs, tax junk food and soda, or mandate exercise classes and healthy school lunches. Controversy also abounds over what causes obesity, whether it can be blamed on socioeconomics, the availability of healthy food, marketing deceptions, genetics, or poor self-control. There is even disagreement over the definition of obesity and whether there is an obesity problem at all.

Less commonly discussed is the role technology is quietly playing in getting people to view exercising, eating healthy, and losing weight as a fun and rewarding game. The growing popularity of various weight loss, exercise, and other behavior-modification smartphone applications, or apps, may offer a surprisingly effective way to curb obesity. At the same time, this approach could cost the state virtually nothing and avoid arguments over what role, if any, the government should play in reducing obesity.

Consider the case of Dan Freedman, who was profiled in a 2012 article in *Atlantic Monthly* about the powerful effect smartphone apps are having on weight loss. Freedman lost about sixty-five pounds and shed a case of type 2 diabetes simply by eating less, eating healthier, and exercising more. Yet he adopted these tried-and-true habits with a twenty-first-century twist: by using various powerful and motivating apps that tracked his food intake and exercise levels. Being able to share his achievements with friends via social networking sites such as Twitter and Facebook compounded his success, as did integrating his devices (such as having his electronic scale wirelessly transmit his weight to his computer) and using high-tech interactive platforms (such as Skype to hold group support meetings with others who were attempting weight loss).

Several sizes later, Freedman is one of millions of people taking their weight loss into their own hands because apps and social networking make it fun, easy, and rewarding to do so. "Early studies of a fast-expanding pool of electronic weight-loss aids suggest that, by allowing people . . . to construct their own regimen on their phone and computer, these tools could be a key to reversing the obesity epidemic," writes *Atlantic* reporter David H. Freedman (Dan's brother). "Now, with the help of our iPhones and a few Facebook friends, we can train ourselves to lead healthier, safer, eco-friendlier, more financially secure, and more productive lives."[1]

Weight Watchers is one immensely popular program that combines behavior-modification principles with technology for fantastic results. Weight Watchers works by quantifying food and making a sort of game out of eating healthy—foods are all assigned points, and a program participant gets a certain number of points per day. They can earn extra points by exercising, or use points by overindulging in high-point foods. They can tinker with portions to spend as few points as possible on the most amount of food (for example, they might eat four egg whites rather than three, because both three and four egg whites are worth a single point) and build recipes exactly to the number of points they have remaining for the day or week. Weight Watchers has an app with which users can quickly and easily track their points and their exercise and share results and recipes with the community, all of whom offer each other motivation, encouragement, and accountability.

A similarly popular and effective weight loss app is called Lose It, which lets users establish an amount of weight to lose by a certain deadline. It then assigns them a daily calorie amount and challenges them to stay at or below it. Tracking food intake is easy and like playing a game: At the grocery store, users can scan packaging barcodes to directly upload a food's nutritional information, and foods are assigned cute little icons. The Lose It app screen features a thermometer-like bar that shows in green the number of calories a user has consumed that day. If the user overeats, the calorie intake goes into the red. An attractive aspect of Lose It

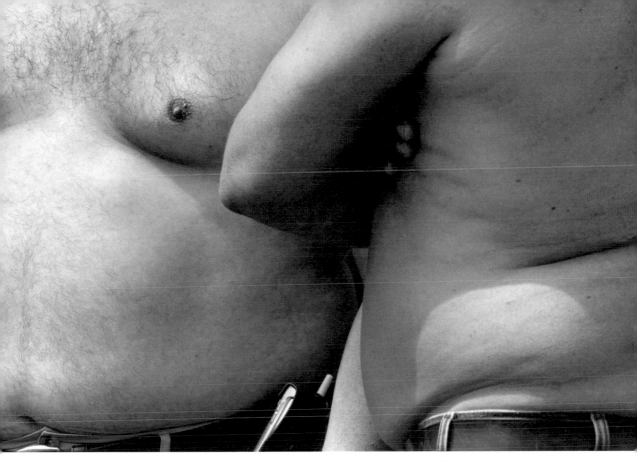

In the twenty-first century, rising rates of obesity have sparked debate over whether the government can, or should, intervene.

is that users can easily see the consequences of their actions or be rewarded for them: For example, they might see that having a second helping of pasta will send them into the red for the day but that walking for thirty minutes after their meal can put them back into the green. Lose It says that 10 million people have used its program since its launch and reports that the average user loses about twelve pounds.

RunKeeper is another popular (and free) health app. It gives people the ability to track and measure their athleticism, in essence offering them personalized data on their exercise habits. RunKeeper shows users how long, far, or fast they have walked, ridden a bike, jogged, hiked, skied, and numerous other activities. It offers their average speed, breaks their progress down per mile, shows a map of the area they covered (for example, their route around a neighborhood), displays their current and average pace, and keeps track of firsts and bests in each activity, sending users a congratulatory e-mail when they run their fastest time or hike their longest distance. "I never particularly liked running," says one RunKeeper user. "It was always boring and I'd give up when I got tired. But I love how RunKeeper quantifies my information for me—I can really see where I went, how far I went, how fast I went, and what I burned. It becomes like a game, a game in which I play against me so I win every time."[2]

Other apps make use of punishment, another behavior modification technique. Consider an app called GymPact, for example, in which users commit to going to the gym at least once per week. If they fail to go, GymPact charges them five dollars. The app uses GPS technology to confirm their presence at the gym and has thus far partnered with more than forty thousand gyms nationwide—more than 70 percent of all gyms. As for all of the five dollar fines collected, GymPact divides the money up among people who keep their gym commitments, rewarding those who go and punishing those who do not. "Behavioral economics show that if you tie cash incentives to things that are concrete and easy to achieve like getting to the gym, it's very effective," says Yifan Zhang, who cofounded the company. "People don't like losing money and it's one of the strongest motivators, much more than winning money."[3]

Together, these various apps and programs represent a complete behavior-modification program that can be downloaded for nearly no cost (excluding the cost of the phone and its monthly service fees) and be managed by the person who has the most stake in his or her own weight loss. Freedman says that if apps, websites, and other high-tech tools could make just a 5 percent dent in America's obesity problem, the United States could save about $15 billion in obesity-related health care costs each year. This is one important reason why health insurance companies are investigating how to encourage the people they insure to use them. "We're very excited about the potential of these tools," says Dr. Don Bradley, chief medical officer of Blue Cross and Blue

Shield of North Carolina. "Up to 70 percent of health-care costs are related to lifestyle. If we can't control those costs, we can't keep our products affordable."[4]

Whether the solution to the obesity problem is simply waiting to be downloaded remains to be seen, however. *Issues That Concern You: Obesity* explores this and other cutting-edge discussions regarding weight loss and health. Approachable and clear pro/con article pairs also explore whether obesity has serious health risks and threatens national security, whether parents of obese children should lose custody of them, and what are the most likely causes and best solutions to obesity. Together they offer students an easily accessible collection of opinions on this issue of ongoing importance.

Notes

1. David H. Freedman, "The Perfected Self," *Atlantic*, June 2012.
2. Connie Bumgarner, interviewed by the author, September 30, 2012.
3. Quoted in Tara Siegel Bernard, "Gym-Pact Fines You for Not Exercising," *Bucks* (blog), *New York Times*, January 2, 2012. http://bucks.blogs.nytimes.com/2012/01/02/gym-pact-fines-you-for-not-exercising/.
4. Quoted in Freedman, "The Perfected Self."

ONE

Obesity Has Serious Health Risks

National Heart, Lung, and Blood Institute

> The following viewpoint was published by the National Heart, Lung, and Blood Institute, a branch of the National Institutes of Health. The author catalogues the many health problems associated with obesity and overweight. These include heart disease, high blood pressure, stroke, and diabetes, all of which are leading causes of death. Being overweight or obese also causes high cholesterol, bone and joint problems, reproductive issues, and other painful, serious disorders such as gallstones. These health problems occur in both obese adults and children. For all of these reasons, the National Heart, Lung, and Blood Institute, along with all of the government's health departments, advocate maintaining a healthy weight.

Being overweight or obese isn't a cosmetic problem. It greatly raises the risk in adults for many diseases and conditions.

Serious Health Concerns

Coronary heart disease. Coronary heart disease (CHD) is a condition in which a substance called plaque (plak) builds up inside the coronary arteries. These arteries supply oxygen-rich blood

"What Are the Health Risks of Overweight and Obesity?," National Heart Lung and Blood Institute, November 1, 2010.

to your heart. Plaque is made up of fat, cholesterol, calcium, and other substances found in the blood.

Plaque can narrow or block the coronary arteries and reduce blood flow to the heart muscle. This can cause angina. (an-JI-nuh or AN-juh-nuh) or a heart attack. (Angina is chest pain or discomfort.)

As your body mass index (BMI) increases, so does your risk of having CHD and a heart attack. Obesity also can lead to heart failure. This is a serious condition in which your heart can't pump enough blood to meet your body's needs.

High blood pressure. Blood pressure is the force of blood pushing against the walls of the arteries as the heart pumps out blood. If this pressure rises and stays high over time, it can damage the

Surgeons perform gastric bypass surgery on an obese patient. Obesity is correlated with serious health risks such as heart disease and diabetes.

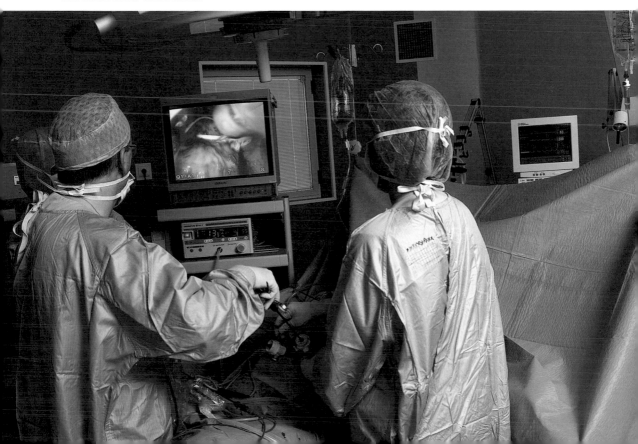

body in many ways. Your chances of having high blood pressure are greater if you're overweight or obese.

Stroke. Being overweight or obese can lead to a buildup of plaque in your arteries. Eventually, an area of plaque can rupture, causing a blood clot to form at the site. If the clot is close to your brain, it can block the flow of blood and oxygen to your brain and cause a stroke. The risk of having a stroke rises as BMI increases.

Type 2 diabetes. Diabetes is a disease in which the body's blood glucose, or blood sugar, level is too high. Normally, the body breaks down food into glucose and then carries it to cells throughout the body. The cells use a hormone called insulin to turn the glucose into energy.

In type 2 diabetes, the body's cells don't use insulin properly. At first, the body reacts by making more insulin. Over time, however, the body can't make enough insulin to control its blood sugar level.

Diabetes is a leading cause of early death, CHD, stroke, kidney disease, and blindness. Most people who have type 2 diabetes are overweight.

Excess Weight Is a Dangerous Precursor

Abnormal blood fats. If you're overweight or obese, you're at increased risk of having abnormal levels of blood fats. These include high levels of triglycerides and LDL ("bad") cholesterol and low levels of HDL ("good") cholesterol.

Abnormal levels of these blood fats are a risk factor for CHD. . . .

Metabolic syndrome. Metabolic syndrome is the name for a group of risk factors linked to overweight and obesity. These risk factors increase your risk of CHD and other health problems, such as diabetes and stroke.

You can develop any one of these risk factors by itself, but they tend to occur together. A diagnosis of metabolic syndrome is made if you have at least three of the following risk factors:

- A large waistline. This also is called abdominal obesity or "having an apple shape." Having extra fat in the waist area is a greater risk factor for CHD than having extra fat in other parts of the body, such as on the hips.

Medical Complications of Obesity

The Centers for Disease Control and Prevention warns that obesity is connected to medical conditions that affect the entire body. This diagram was adapted from Yale University Rudd Center for Food Policy and Obesity.

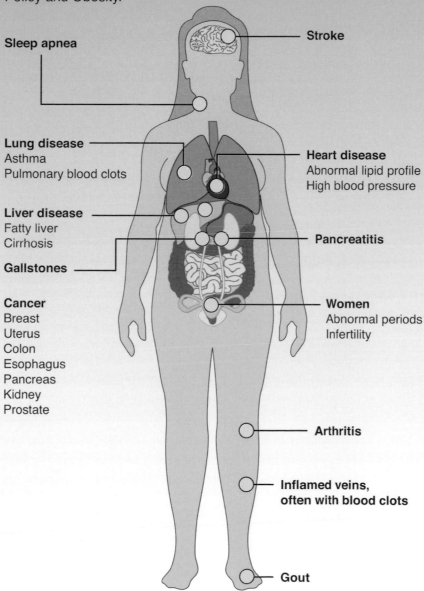

Sleep apnea

Stroke

Lung disease
Asthma
Pulmonary blood clots

Heart disease
Abnormal lipid profile
High blood pressure

Liver disease
Fatty liver
Cirrhosis

Pancreatitis

Gallstones

Cancer
Breast
Uterus
Colon
Esophagus
Pancreas
Kidney
Prostate

Women
Abnormal periods
Infertility

Arthritis

**Inflamed veins,
often with blood clots**

Gout

- A higher than normal triglyceride level (or you're on medicine to treat high triglycerides).
- A lower than normal HDL cholesterol level (or you're on medicine to treat low HDL cholesterol).
- Higher than normal blood pressure (or you're on medicine to treat high blood pressure).
- Higher than normal fasting blood sugar (or you're on medicine to treat diabetes).

Cancer. Being overweight or obese raises the risk of colon, breast, endometrial [uterine], and gallbladder cancers.

Osteoarthritis. Osteoarthritis is a common joint problem of the knees, hips, and lower back. The condition occurs if the tissue that protects the joints wears away. Extra weight can put more pressure and wear on joints, causing pain.

Sleep apnea. Sleep apnea is a common disorder in which you have one or more pauses in breathing or shallow breaths while you sleep.

A person who has sleep apnea may have more fat stored around the neck. This can narrow the airway, making it hard to breathe.

Reproductive problems. Obesity can cause menstrual irregularity and infertility in women.

Gallstones. Gallstones are hard pieces of stone-like material that form in the gallbladder. They're mostly made of cholesterol. Gallstones can cause abdominal or back pain.

People who are overweight or obese are at increased risk of having gallstones. Also, being overweight may result in an enlarged gallbladder that doesn't work right.

Problems in Children and Teens. Overweight and obesity also increase the health risks for children and teens. Type 2 diabetes once was rare in American children, but an increasing number of children are developing the disease.

Also, overweight children are more likely to become overweight or obese as adults, with the same disease risks.

TWO

The Health Risks of Obesity Have Been Exaggerated

Patrick Basham and John Luik

Obesity is not as dangerous as policy makers and some "crusaders" would have people believe, argue Patrick Basham and John Luik in the following viewpoint. They discuss a prominent study that found that being fat around one's midsection does not increase a person's risk of having a heart attack. Basham and Luik say this is one of many studies that prove wrong the conventional wisdom that being overweight or obese can kill. In reality, they claim, there is no good scientific evidence linking overweight or obesity with death. They suggest that the obesity-death link has been perpetuated by politicians or activists who have a political agenda. Basham and Luik urge people to critically evaluate claims about obesity's health risks, and they conclude that being fat does not kill.

Basham is a Cato Institute adjunct scholar and the director of the Democracy Institute, where Luik is a senior fellow. Together they are the authors of the book *Diet Nation: Exposing the Obesity Crusade*.

Since the anti-obesity campaign is allegedly motivated by scientific findings, it would seem reasonable and prudent to make doubly sure that those claims are factual and trustworthy. Yet, we continue to find that the case against obesity is significantly flawed. Not only are the claims of an obesity epidemic often wildly exaggerated, but the science linking weight to unfavourable mortality outcomes is also frequently nonexistent or distorted.

BMI No Relation to Mortality

For example, a study published in *The Lancet* medical journal last week [in March 2011] has driven an empirical stake through the heart of the conventional wisdom that being 'apple shaped' increases one's risk of a heart attack. The study found the risk of heart attack was not increased by fat being concentrated around the waist, which flatly contradicts earlier research that said overweight people with fat deposits in the middle of their body—or, to put it another way, having apple-shaped bodies—were three times as likely to suffer heart attacks than those with more generally distributed fat.

Who does and does not have an apple-shaped body is determined by measuring the waist-to-hip ratio—that is, comparing the distance around the hips and the distance around the waist to measure what is known as "central obesity'. Someone with a bulging middle is 'apple-shaped', someone with a narrower waist but fatter hips and bottom is described as 'pear-shaped'.

The *Lancet* study was conducted by a research team led by Cambridge University's John Danesh, which studied 220,000 people over the course of a decade. According to Professor Danesh, the study found that, 'Whether assessed singly or in combination, body-mass index (BMI), waist circumference, and waist-to-hip ratio do not improve prediction of first-onset cardiovascular disease when additional information exists on blood pressure, history of diabetes, and cholesterol measures'.

As Danesh suggests, other researchers have suggested concentrating on a measurement of the waist alone, while many cling to BMI, which calculates obesity based upon a weight-to-height ratio. Because of its easy applicability, BMI is universally used in officially defining obesity, despite its manifest shortcomings. The BMI is wholly arbitrary and has no scientifically valid connection with mortality.

The Manufactured Obesity "Epidemic"

'Obesity crusaders' are what we call the individuals who manufactured the obesity-epidemic story in the first place and continue, through application of inherently flawed instruments, such as BMI and apple-body shapes, to misinform the public. They are a relatively small group of public-health officials in the US, the UK [United Kingdom], the EU [European Union], and the World Health Organisation, assorted academics (very many with

A study published in the Lancet *medical journal found that the risk of heart attack was not increased in people who have fat concentrated around the waist.*

What's Your Body Mass Index?

Body mass index (BMI) is calculated using a person's weight and height. Although the government says normal BMI is 24 or less, others argue one can be healthy at higher BMIs.

	BMI	\multicolumn{19}{c}{Height (inches)}																	
		58	59	60	61	62	63	64	65	66	67	68	69	70	71	72	73	74	75	76
Normal	19	91	94	97	100	104	107	110	114	118	121	125	128	132	136	140	144	148	152	156
	20	96	99	102	106	109	113	116	120	124	127	131	135	139	143	147	151	155	160	164
	21	100	104	107	111	115	118	122	126	130	134	138	142	146	150	154	159	163	168	172
	22	105	109	112	116	120	124	128	132	136	140	144	149	153	157	162	166	171	176	180
	23	110	114	118	122	126	130	134	138	142	146	151	155	160	165	169	174	179	184	189
	24	115	119	123	127	131	135	140	144	148	153	158	162	167	172	177	182	186	192	197
Overweight	25	119	124	128	132	136	141	145	150	155	159	164	169	174	179	184	189	194	200	205
	26	124	128	133	137	142	146	151	156	161	166	171	176	181	186	191	197	202	208	213
	27	129	133	138	143	147	152	157	162	167	172	177	182	188	193	199	204	210	216	221
	28	134	138	143	148	153	158	163	168	173	178	184	189	195	200	206	212	218	224	230
	29	138	143	148	153	158	163	169	174	179	185	190	196	202	208	213	219	225	232	238
Obese	30	143	148	153	158	164	169	174	180	186	191	197	203	209	215	221	227	233	240	246
	31	148	152	158	164	169	175	180	186	192	198	203	209	216	222	228	235	241	248	254
	32	153	158	163	169	175	180	186	192	198	204	210	216	222	229	235	242	249	256	263
	33	158	163	168	174	180	186	192	198	204	211	216	223	229	236	242	250	256	264	271
	34	162	168	174	180	186	191	197	204	210	217	223	230	236	243	250	257	264	272	279
	35	167	173	179	185	191	197	204	210	216	223	230	236	243	250	258	265	272	279	287
	36	172	178	184	190	196	203	209	216	223	230	236	243	250	257	265	272	280	287	295
	37	177	183	189	195	202	208	215	222	229	236	243	250	257	265	272	280	287	295	304
	38	181	188	194	201	207	214	221	228	235	242	249	257	264	272	279	288	295	303	312
	39	186	193	199	206	213	220	227	234	241	249	256	263	271	279	287	295	303	311	320
Extreme Obesity	40	191	198	204	211	218	225	232	240	247	255	262	270	278	286	294	302	311	319	328
	41	196	203	209	217	224	231	238	246	253	261	269	277	285	293	302	310	319	327	336
	42	201	208	215	222	229	237	244	252	260	268	276	284	292	301	309	318	326	335	344
	43	205	212	220	227	235	242	250	258	266	274	282	291	299	308	316	325	334	343	353
	44	210	217	225	232	240	248	256	264	272	280	289	297	306	315	324	333	342	351	361
	45	215	222	230	238	246	254	262	270	278	287	295	304	313	322	331	340	350	359	369
	46	220	227	235	243	251	259	267	276	284	293	302	311	320	329	338	348	358	367	377
	47	224	232	240	248	256	265	273	282	291	299	308	318	327	338	346	355	365	375	385
	48	229	237	245	254	262	270	279	288	297	306	315	324	334	343	353	363	373	383	394
	49	234	242	250	259	267	278	285	294	303	312	322	331	341	351	361	371	381	391	402
	50	239	247	255	264	273	282	291	300	309	319	328	338	348	358	388	378	389	399	410
	51	244	252	261	269	278	287	296	306	315	325	335	345	355	365	375	386	396	407	418
	52	248	257	266	275	284	293	302	312	322	331	341	351	362	372	383	393	404	415	426
	53	253	262	271	280	289	299	308	318	328	338	348	358	369	379	390	401	412	423	435
	54	258	267	278	285	295	304	314	324	334	344	254	365	376	386	397	408	420	431	443

(Body Weight (pounds))

Taken from: *Clinical Guidelines on the Identification, Evaluation, and Treatment of Overweight and Obesity in Adults: The Evidence Report*. National Institutes of Health, 2012.

close ties to the weight-loss and pharmaceutical industry), the International Obesity Task Force, and a collection of so-called public-interest science groups.

How are these obesity crusaders reacting to the unambiguously good news published in *The Lancet*? Surely, they rejoice at the fact there is one less thing for a health-conscious population to fret over? No, they are not in celebratory mood. Quite the contrary. The obesity crusaders did not waste any time on the New Good News; after all, the Old-Time Religion continues to serve them so well.

Above all, the obesity crusaders stress that obesity is still bad for you. The British Heart Foundation's associate medical director, Dr Mike Knapton, said it was clear that no matter how you measure it, obesity is bad for your heart. '[M]easuring our waist or checking our BMI are both quick and easy ways we can check our health at home', he said.

Strangely, the obesity crusaders remain unaware that there is an absence of scientific evidence to support their assertions: firstly, that overweight and obesity increase one's mortality risks; and secondly, that the overweight and moderately obese should lose weight because such loss will improve their health and lower their risk of heart disease.

In fact, the obesity crusaders' assertions about weight and longevity ignore 40 years' worth of international data that suggest obesity is not a cause of premature mortality. Many studies for different disease outcomes have demonstrated that the effect of both diet and physical activity are independent of the effect of BMI or various measures of body size or fat.

Distorting Science to Pursue an Agenda

There is little credible scientific evidence that supports the claims that being overweight or obese leads to an early death. For example, Katherine Flegal of the Centers for Disease Control and Prevention found that in the US population there were more premature deaths among those who are normal weight than those who are overweight. Indeed, in this study, Americans who were overweight were those most likely to live the longest.

In the *American Journal of Public Health,* Jerome Gronniger found that men in the 'normal' weight category exhibited a mortality rate as high as that of men in the moderately obese category; men in the 'overweight' category clearly had the lowest mortality risk.

Moreover, a recent study published in the *American Journal of Clinical Nutrition* that looked at alternative measures of obesity, such as percentage of body fat, skin-fold thickness, waist circumference, and waist-hip ratio, found even less scientific support for the alleged fat-equals-early-death thesis. The authors report that for the intermediate level of each of the alternative measures of obesity, there was a negative link with mortality. In other words, those with a higher waist circumference or a higher percentage of body fat had lower mortality rates.

All of which should serve to remind us that the success of the obesity crusade rests not on the truth of its science, but on the way in which the obesity entrepreneurs use that science to change policy. Going forward, better policymaking will require, at a minimum, a far greater appreciation of the way in which science and its findings are both misrepresented and used by the obesity crusaders to distort the regulatory process.

Indeed, the last thing that the obesity crusaders would wish is to have rigorous science discount the circumstantial, indeed largely nonexistent, evidence on which the obesity epidemic is based. As the new study in *The Lancet* illustrates, the available knowledge is sufficient merely to label as reckless any crusade by self-appointed and self-serving public health authorities that profess to know what they plainly do not.

THREE

Obesity Threatens National Security

Mission: Readiness

> Mission: Readiness is an organization made up of more than a hundred retired generals, admirals, and senior enlisted leaders. In the following report, it argues that many young Americans are too fat to qualify for military service. To be eligible for service, one must be in good enough shape to deal with the many physical demands of the military environment. Yet America's youth are so overweight and out of shape that many cannot pass the physical exams required for entry into the military, Mission: Readiness claims. If this trend continues, the author warns, there will not be enough people to serve in the military, which will weaken the armed forces and threaten the country's ability to defend itself. They urge lawmakers, school officials, and others to reduce children's access to junk food and make exercise a higher priority so that the United States will not be short on physically fit soldiers.

Military leaders have stood up before to make sure America's youth had proper nutrition for a healthy start in life. During World War II, the military discovered that at least 40 percent of rejected recruits were turned away for reasons related to poor nutrition. Stunted growth from inadequate nutrition and poor health was so common that the young men who made it into the military during World War II were more than an inch and a half shorter, on average, than young American men today. After the war ended, General Lewis Hershey, the military's Selective Service Director, delivered testimony that helped win passage of the National School Lunch Program. The National School Lunch Program, established in 1946, helped improve the health and well-being of our nation by making sure children across America had access to healthful meals at school.

An Epidemic That Threatens National Security

Once again, America's retired military leaders are alerting Congress to a threat to national security. The basic fact is that too many young American men and women are too fat to fight.

The Army's estimate of who is too heavy to join the military: The Army's Accessions Command, which carries the responsibility for recruiting and the initial training of new Army recruits, estimates that over 27 percent of all Americans 17 to 24 years of age—over nine million young men and women—are too heavy to join the military if they want to do so. The Army's estimate is based on the national survey conducted for it by the Lewin Group in 2005. The estimate uses a weight-for-height cutoff that allows somewhat higher weights than the cutoff used by civilian organizations, such as the National Institutes of Health.

The number of recruits actually turned away after taking their physicals has risen dramatically in the last decade. If a young man or woman seeking to enter the military is otherwise qualified but is obviously too heavy, a recruiter will not schedule a trip for that person to the regional Military Entrance Processing Center. But between 1995 and 2008, the military had 140,000 individuals who showed up at the centers for processing but failed their entrance physicals because they were too heavy. Being overweight is now by far the leading medical reason for rejection, and between 1995 and 2008, the proportion of potential recruits who failed their physicals each year because they were overweight rose nearly 70 percent.

First Lady Michelle Obama (center) meets with soldiers about the "Go for Green" program, which aims to reduce obesity problems in the US military.

The CDC's national and state estimates for who is overweight or obese: The CDC [Centers for Disease Control and Prevention] uses a more standard cutoff in their definition of who is overweight. Using that cutoff and their own Behavior Risk Factor Surveillance System data collected every year, the CDC found that 42 percent of young adults 18 to 24 years were either overweight or obese. That equals eleven million young adults. To be within the healthy weight range, those young people would have to lose almost 400 million total pounds.

Many Americans Too Fat to Fight

Whichever measurement is used—the military's or the CDC's—it is beyond question that too many young Americans are overweight or obese. Within just a ten-year period ending in 2008, the number of states reporting that 40 percent or more of their young adults were overweight or obese went from just one state, Kentucky, to 39 states. And in three states—Kentucky, Mississippi and Alabama—over 50 percent of young adults had become overweight or obese within the decade.

Too Fat to Fight

At least 9 million seventeen- to twenty-four-year-olds in the United States are too fat to serve in the military. That is 27 percent of all young adults. Over a ten-year period, the number of states with 40 percent or more of their young adults who were overweight or obese went from one to thirty-nine. In three states, more than half of young adults are overweight. These statistics were derived from the Centers for Disease Control and Prevention, Behavioral Risk Factor Surveillance System.

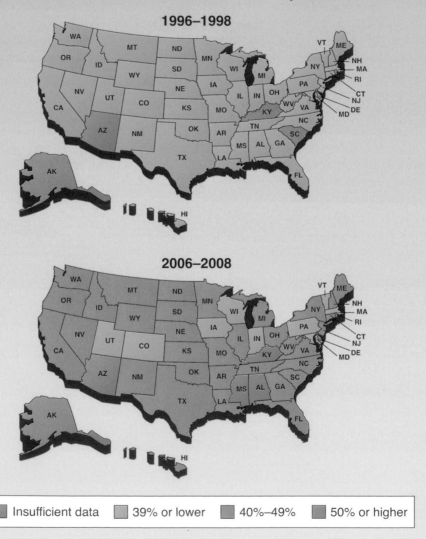

1996–1998

2006–2008

Insufficient data   39% or lower   40%–49%   50% or higher

Taken from: Mission: Readiness. *Too Fat to Fight: Retired Military Leaders Want Junk Food out of America's Schools,* April 28, 2010, p. 1.

Childhood obesity rates have accelerated faster than adult obesity rates. Over the past 30 years, while adult rates of obesity have doubled, childhood obesity rates have tripled. The *Journal of the American Dietary Association* reports that "Almost one-third of American children—nearly 23 million children and teens—are either overweight or obese." Largely because of this epidemic of obesity, today's children may be the first generation of Americans to live shorter lives than their parents.

Seventy-five percent of Americans 17 to 24 years old are unable to join the military for one or more reasons. A quarter of young Americans are currently not graduating from high school on time. Another 10 percent of Americans cannot join the military because of their criminal records. Some have other disqualifiers keeping them out and some have multiple reasons they cannot join.

When weight problems are combined with educational deficits, criminal records, and other disqualifiers such as asthma or drug abuse, 75 percent of Americans 17 to 24 years old are unable to join the military for one or more reasons. The military will need to have more fit young men and women if it is going to find enough recruits with the excellent qualifications needed for a modern military. . . .

Obesity a Problem Within the Military, Too

Unfortunately, the impact of weight problems on the military does not stop with those turned away. Every year, the military discharges over 1,200 first-term enlistees before their contracts are up because of weight problems; the military must then recruit and train their replacements at a cost of $50,000 for each man or woman, thus spending more than $60 million a year. That figure pales in comparison, however, to the cost of treating the obesity-related problems of military personnel and their families under the military's health care system, TRICARE, or the cost of treating obesity-related problems under the veterans' health care system.

Although estimates of the current costs of obesity vary, the costs associated with obesity-related heart disease, diabetes, cancer and other health problems are clearly increasing. The American Public Health Association projects, for example, that "left unchecked, obesity will add nearly $344 billion to the nation's annual health care costs by 2018 and account for more than 21 percent of health care spending."

According to the most recent national surveys by the CDC, there are indications that childhood and adult obesity rates may be leveling off. But there is no consensus on whether this is just a plateau before rates increase again, or it is the beginning of a reversal of this epidemic. In any case, the current levels of obesity are much too high. . . .

Our Health and Security Are at Risk

To begin reversing the epidemic of childhood obesity, Congress should:

1) *Get the junk food and high-calorie beverages out of our schools* by allowing the Secretary of Agriculture to adopt the Institute of Medicine standards for what can be served or marketed in schools.

2) *Increase funding for the school lunch programs.* This funding will help deliver healthier, lower-calorie meals to more poor children who are already eligible to receive them and to others from millions of families that purchase the meals. That can help the students control their weight now and—if the meals are more appetizing—reinforce the message that they can successfully adopt healthier life-long habits.

3) *Support the development, testing and deployment of proven public-health interventions* that can deliver the education and encouragement children and their parents need to adopt healthier life-long eating and exercise habits.

The United States military stands ready to protect the American people, but if our nation does not help ensure that future generations grow up to be healthy and fit, that will become increasingly difficult. The health of our children and our national security are at risk. America must act decisively.

FOUR

Lack of Personal Responsibility Causes Obesity

Deborah Coddington

> Obesity is primarily an issue of personal responsibility, argues Deborah Coddington in the following viewpoint. She says that people are fat simply because they eat fatty foods and fail to exercise. No one is forcing them to eat poorly, she claims; there is no conspiracy by food manufacturers to make people overindulge in their products. Rather, some people are fat because they lack willpower and personal accountability. Coddington says it is insulting to cast fat people as victims of the food industry. It takes away their agency and puts the government in the unwelcome position of deciding for people what they should and should not eat. Coddington says we must not view the obese as helpless victims who have no control over their figures; rather, we must hold them accountable for their poor choices and blame no one for their obesity but themselves.
>
> Coddington is a journalist for the *New Zealand Herald*.

It's official: we're a nation of idiots who can't make decisions to save ourselves or take responsibility for our problems.

That's according to two academics from Otago University, researchers in public health, Dr Gabrielle Jenkin and Penny Field, who specialise in the obesity epidemic.

Interviewed this week [in January 2012] by Kathryn Ryan on National Radio, Field tossed off a comment which sent me into deep despair. Obesity, she said, was "not a problem with individual choice and self-discipline, which we've proved successfully doesn't work".

Instead it's the fault of "big institutions and the market".

The obese as victims. It's come to this. Fat people are mentally incapable of choosing what's right and wrong when it comes to putting food in their mouths.

In New Zealand, 63 per cent of us are overweight or obese, so, by Field and Jenkin's reckoning, the brain power of 63 per cent of the New Zealand population is on par with labradors or ponies which can't stop eating themselves to death.

Government needed to do something, they complained, starting with more regulation of advertising, particularly on children's television.

What I interpret from this is that, zombie-like, our children are brainwashed into wanting bad food.

Ceding Personal Responsibility to the Government

In turn, they demand this bad food from pliable parents who can't say no and, too dumb to discern healthy food from bad food, meekly buy that which "the market" or "the big institutions" persuade them to buy.

How conspiratorial.

If this is the case, we might as well give up. The Government could just nationalise all food outlets, supermarkets, dairies, green-grocers and farmers' markets and the Minister for Food Safety could have an army of inspectors to ensure we only eat healthy food, with no fat or sugar.

And why stop there? Why not have the Government issue us all with packed lunches every day? After all, it's not just our children who are obese.

Every day, in every town and city, we all see fat people waddling along, heaving themselves into planes and cars, but are we allowed to comment on this, the way we were encouraged to

Americans Think People Bear Responsibility for Being Obese

A 2012 poll found the majority of Americans think obesity results from making poor personal choices.

Question: More American adults and children are obese today than at any time in the past. What do you think is the main reason for this?

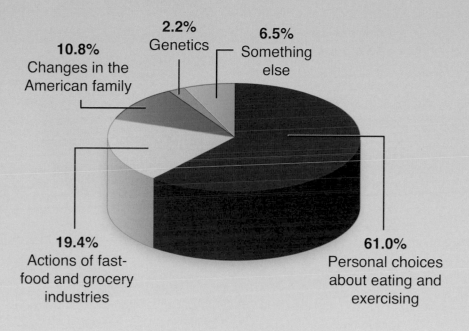

2.2% Genetics

6.5% Something else

10.8% Changes in the American family

19.4% Actions of fast-food and grocery industries

61.0% Personal choices about eating and exercising

Taken from: Reuters/Ipsos Poll: Obesity's Stigma in America, May 7–10, 2012.

shame smokers into quitting (who also cost taxpayers dearly in terms of the public health bill)?

No, and now we know why. According to Jenkin and Field, they can't help it. It's all the fault of the food industry, a force to be reckoned with in terms of its well-funded and slick lobbying, according to these academics.

In 2006, Jenkin sat through the select committee inquiry into obesity, chaired by Green MP [Green Party member of Parliament] Sue Kedgley, and concluded the food industry has far too much influence on policy-making when it comes to trying to curb obesity.

Some people believe a person's health is their own responsibility, not the government's.

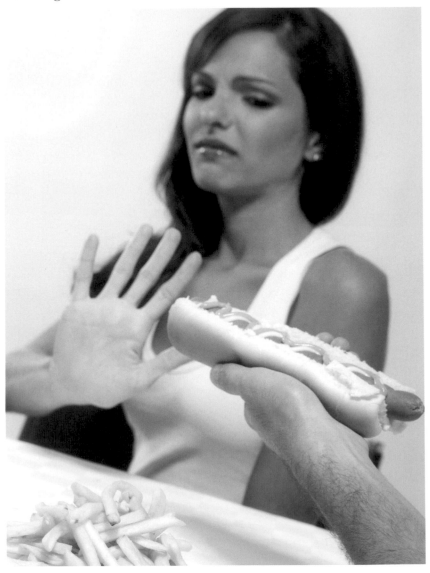

You could easily have substituted the words "tobacco industry" for "food industry" in this interview, such was the palpable disgust these women had for food manufacturers. Anyone would think the food industry conspires to make us obese.

Hold People Accountable for Their Figures

Haven't they forgotten something? We actually need food to survive. The makers of all foodstuffs—even hamburgers, pies, pizzas, fizzy drinks and cakes—don't hold guns to our heads and force-feed us, as if we're foie gras geese [specially fattened to make a gourmet spread from their livers].

And I'm no academic, but here's a simple question on choice. If fat people can say "no" to a brisk walk and a salad at lunchtime, then surely they can give the same answer to an invitation to Burger King?

This attitude from academics is patronising and silly. Yes, there are some grossly obese people for whom stomach-stapling is the resort, so impossible is it for them to lose weight, but they're a small minority.

For the rest of us, choice and self-discipline most definitely does work. Eat less food, whatever that may be, and exercise more. If we jettison that weapon in the weight-control battle, what next? Budgeting? Fighting fraud? Why bother prosecuting directors of finance companies who fail to protect the savings of investors by exercising self-discipline and choice, but excuse themselves by saying they were victims of the global financial crisis?

Jenkin's final words were that the food industry needs to be held accountable for obesity. No. Individuals need to be held accountable and stop blaming food and its makers for their problem.

FIVE

Obesity Is Not Related to Personal Responsibility Alone

David J. Linden

Obesity is not merely a matter of willpower or personal responsibility, argues David J. Linden in the following viewpoint. He explains that complex genetic and biological processes inform a person's weight. Obese people are wired differently than thin people and thus have a harder time losing weight and keeping it off. To suggest that obese people should just eat less and exercise more vastly oversimplifies the problem, argues Linden. Obese people cannot control their genes or the neurological processes that determine how they eat and process food. It is deeply cruel and unfair to characterize obese people as lazy sloths who lack willpower, he concludes. The truth of obesity is much more complex and out of their hands than that, he adds.

Linden is a neuroscience professor at the Johns Hopkins University School of Medicine and the author of the book *The Compass of Pleasure*.

Why can't that obese man just eat less and exercise more? He lacks willpower, surely.

It's a value judgment that is made countless times a day, in our lives and in the news media. But these attitudes are destructive, cruel and scientifically wrong.

Obesity Is Not Just About Willpower

Willpower is a fine thing, but the best intentions of this man's conscious mind—indeed, all of ours—must struggle against tens of thousands of years of evolutionary history. Simply put, our bodies contain appetite-control circuits that make it very hard to lose a lot of weight and keep it off.

Body fat secretes a hormone called leptin, and this hormone is carried by circulating blood and passes into the brain to reduce appetite. When we lose weight, less body fat means that less leptin gets to the brain. This causes a strong subconscious drive to eat and makes foods—particularly fatty and sweet foods—more pleasurable when consumed. The more weight that is lost, the stronger this drive will be.

A researcher analyzes fat cells. The size of fat cells in offspring is influenced by genes inherited from the mother.

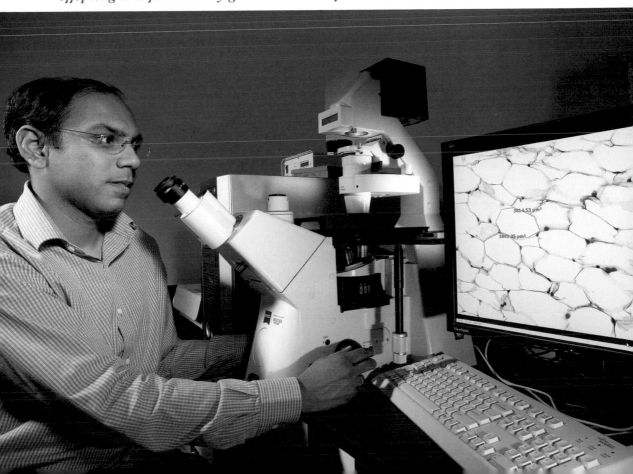

While moderate weight loss can be maintained through willful monitoring of food intake and exercise, and dramatic weight loss can be achieved temporarily, it is very difficult for most people to maintain an extreme loss of weight over the long term because of this leptin-feedback system.

Even liposuction is only a temporary fix: Removal of fat from the body reduces levels of leptin, thereby increasing appetite. This is the sad yet unavoidable truth that the multibillion dollar weight-loss industry—from diet book authors to weight-loss reality shows to manufactured "diet foods"—doesn't want you to know.

Unfair and Cruel Stereotyping

The ugly flip side of the notion that dramatic sustained weight loss is within everyone's grasp is the idea that if you're overweight, it's just because you're just a lazy slug.

Depicting an overweight character in a TV sitcom or a film is an easy shorthand: This person is sloppy, unsexy and lacking in self-control. Not like us.

Here's the root of the problem: Evolution is slow, but cultures and technology can change quickly. For most of our human history we rarely had access to sweet or fatty foods. We belonged to hunter-gatherer societies and burned a lot of energy in everyday tasks. In that distant past, it made sense to have an appetite-control system in the brain that made eating those sweet, fatty foods highly pleasurable. This behavior was useful to pack on the pounds when these energy-rich foods were available so that you wouldn't starve during the next protracted famine.

Today, when we try to lose large amounts of weight and keep it off, we are fighting against an evolutionary history geared to a food landscape that no longer exists. Our appetites are calibrated to a diet of roots and shoots and very little meats or sweets—not the McDonald's Extra Value Meal and a 64-ounce soda.

But why, given access to unlimited calories, as is the case for most of us North Americans, will only some people become obese? Is there evidence for a genetic component, or is it all the result of environmental factors?

A Genetic Explanation for Obesity?

Studies continue to discover genetic regions associated with obesity. Some genes affect appetite control and others may play a role in metabolism. Studies on obese families from different ethnic groups have identified common genetic regions linked to obesity on chromosomes 2, 3, 5, 6, 7, 10, and 20.

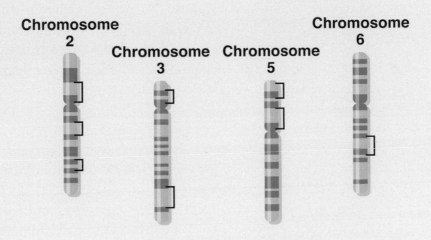

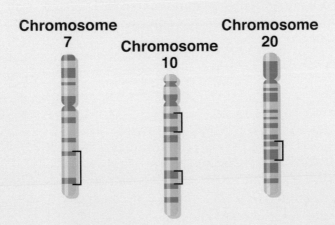

For a significant fraction of the world's population, environmental concerns are overriding: If you don't have access to sufficient nutrition, you can't become obese. Likewise, many cultural factors as well as aspects of an individual's life history also come into play. Stress also has an important role in appetite that is produced by stress hormone action in the brain.

Genetics Play a Huge Role

However, surprisingly, data from adopted twin studies indicate that in the United States, about 80% of the variation in body weight is determined by genes. Again, that's about the same degree of heritability as a characteristic such as height, and much greater than that for other conditions that we now clearly regard as running in families, including breast cancer, schizophrenia and heart disease. Yet, we don't typically call a heart disease sufferer a weak-willed loser.

Brain-imaging studies of obese patients indicate that a genetically determined alteration in the brain's pleasure circuitry makes them crave food more while getting less pleasure from eating than those in a lean control group.

The idea that eating is an entirely conscious and voluntary behavior is deeply rooted in our culture. When we show compassion to the overweight, we must confront the difficult truth that we are not pure creatures of free will. We are—all of us—subject to powerful subconscious forces that influence our behavior.

It's not just that fat guy.

SIX

Poverty Is Linked to Obesity

Susan Blumenthal

In the following viewpoint Susan Blumenthal argues that poverty contributes to obesity. Poor neighborhoods lack stores that sell healthy foods, in part because these foods are more expensive. Rather than supermarkets, many low-income neighborhoods have fast-food restaurants or convenience stores, neither of which offer residents healthy choices. Poor neighborhoods also tend to be dangerous, which means their residents have fewer opportunities to play outdoors or exercise. For all of these reasons, Blumenthal says that people's communities deeply affect their health, and she is not surprised that low-income people are more likely to be obese. To break the poverty-obesity link, she concludes that poor communities must get funding to host affordable, healthful-food stores, community gardens, safe parks, walking paths, and other health-promoting centers.

Blumenthal is the public-health editor of the *Huffington Post*, an online newspaper, and has been a leader of various government health programs for more than twenty years.

There is finally a glimmer of hope in the fight against obesity, a critical public health and economic crisis burdening our nation. After several decades of steep upswings, the Centers for Disease Control and Prevention (CDC) recently reported that obesity rates in the U.S. may be stabilizing, with no significant change in prevalence over the past two years for children. However, experts also warn of the major challenges ahead in the battle against obesity in America.

Despite the apparent recent leveling-off in childhood obesity rates, the prevalence of obesity nonetheless remains high, with more than one-third of adults and almost 17 percent of youth obese in 2009–2010. There are also significant concerns about the health and economic consequences that result from obesity-related complications. Diabetes, coronary heart disease, stroke, cancer, and osteoarthritis are just some of the illnesses associated with obesity that impose human suffering as well as significant medical costs. In 2008, obesity-related medical expenses reached $147 billion, double the amount spent 10 years ago. This figure is projected to rise to $344 billion by 2018, underscoring the magnitude of the economic threat, as an estimated 50 million days of employment and $150 billion in productivity are lost annually in the U.S. due to overweight and obesity-related chronic conditions.

Low-Income Children More Likely to Be Obese than High-Income Children

To address this health crisis, attention must be focused on a key issue that lies at the core of the epidemic: the social inequities of obesity. A significant body of scientific evidence links poverty with higher rates of obesity. Findings from the National Health and Nutrition Examination Survey (NHANES), the most comprehensive study conducted thus far to document the nutritional status of the U.S. population, has found that low-income children and adolescents are more likely to be obese than their higher income counterparts. Additionally, reports have shown a higher prevalence of obesity among low-income adults. One study revealed that more than one-third of adults who earn less than

Among men, there is no significant trend between education level and obesity prevalence. Among women, however, obesity prevalence increases as education decreases.

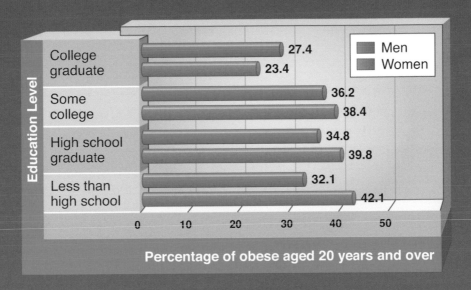

Taken from: National Center for Health Statistics (NCHS) Data Brief no. 50, December 2010.

$15,000 annually were obese, as compared to 25 percent [one-fourth] of those who earn more than $50,000 a year. Visually, a compelling correlation emerges when comparing maps detailing poverty and obesity rates in the U.S.

Major contributing factors to the disproportional impact of obesity on low income populations in America include the barriers faced by people living in poverty in accessing healthy foods, a lack of nutrition education, a dearth of safe environments for physical activity and recreation, and food marketing targeted to this population. Population level data have shown that diet quality follows a socioeconomic gradient. People with higher socioeconomic status (SES) are more likely to consume whole grains, lean meats, fish, low-fat dairy products, and fresh vegetables and fruit. In contrast, lower SES is associated with the consumption of more refined grains and added fats.

Simply stated, families with limited economic resources may turn to food with poor nutritional quality because it is cheaper and more accessible. Lack of physical activity is another commonly-cited problem fueling the obesity epidemic in America. Some low-income families live in neighborhoods

Many low-income neighborhoods lack stores that sell healthy foods and instead are overrun by fast-food restaurants and convenience stores.

where it is dangerous to play outside, reducing opportunities for both children and adults to exercise. Furthermore, many low-income communities lack access to fresh and nutritious food. Instead of a supermarket, these neighborhoods may have an abundance of fast-food retailers and corner stores that are stocked with products high in fat and low in nutrients. Additionally, low-income families are often targeted by food marketers with advertisements encouraging the consumption of nutrient-poor foods. In this environment, children in low-income families are especially hard hit, as evidence demonstrates that consistent exposure to such advertising increases the likelihood of adopting unhealthy dietary practices.

Communities Impact Health

Therefore, in developing a strategy to reverse the obesity epidemic in America, a comprehensive "health in all policies" approach must be implemented. A roadmap to reverse obesity will not only tackle health and nutrition issues, but also focus on the underlying social and environmental factors that contribute to this public health problem. Decades of scientific research have revealed that our health habits and environments—the choices people make regarding tobacco use, alcohol, food, and exercise, and the communities in which they live with their transportation systems, workplaces, grocery stores, and schools—all impact health. Thus, a broad range of strategies are needed to address the individual, social and environmental factors and their interactions that affect people's health-related behaviors.

At the national level, several initiatives have been launched to address these fundamental issues. The Affordable Care Act 2010 has mandated inclusion of menu labeling in restaurants and on vending machines, the Healthy Hunger-Free Kids Act 2010 has set nutrition standards for foods served in schools and child care facilities, and the increase in the number of Baby Friendly hospitals has expanded efforts to promote breastfeeding. Furthermore, First Lady Michelle Obama's Let's Move Campaign is mobilizing all sectors of society to get involved in reversing childhood obesity rates within a generation. As part of this initiative, the Child Care State Challenge is encouraging the adoption of voluntary standards for physical activity, limits on screen time, healthy beverages, and promoting the availability of healthy foods in child care settings.

Promoting Healthy Behaviors in Low-Income Areas

At the community level, new affordable housing neighborhoods like Greenbridge, Washington (located in King County near Seattle) are being designed and built as models for creating an environment that promotes healthy diets and active lifestyles for their residents. In this predominantly immigrant community where more than 15 languages are spoken, more than 54 percent of adults are overweight or obese, and more than 85 percent of adolescents in grades 8, 10, and 12 do not meet the physical activity recommendations set by the federal government. Supported by Healthy Kids, Healthy Communities (HKHC), a national program funded by the Robert Wood Johnson Foundation that promotes community-based solutions, Greenbridge focuses on shaping the environment to encourage healthy behaviors among families, with special attention to children who are at the highest risk. Thus far, a comprehensive set of measures has been put in place to foster the development of a healthier community. In addition to an elementary school, a Head Start program, and a Boy and Girls Club, this new affordable housing initiative offers community gardens to grow fresh fruits and vegetables, a library, as well as play areas, parks, and walking paths. A food bank, a public health clinic, and a community center that provides free exercise classes are located just a few blocks away.

This integrative approach has turned a troubled neighborhood into a welcoming place to live. This new community emphasizes the importance of cultivating a nurturing environment for youth, especially as children and adolescents constitute over a quarter of the neighborhood's population.

Initiatives like this one that involve not only individuals but the entire family and community provide a model for how to

Obesity and Income Levels, 2005–2008

Obesity's relationship to poverty is unclear and varies. Among men, obesity prevalence is generally similar at all income levels, with a tendency to be slightly higher at higher income levels. Among women, obesity prevalence increases as income decreases.

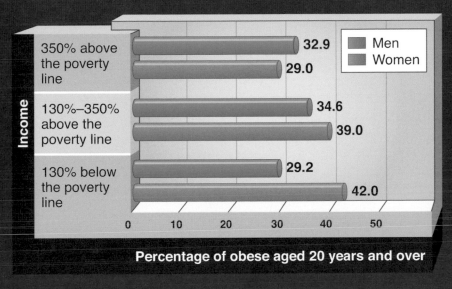

Men
Women

Income	Men	Women
350% above the poverty line	32.9	29.0
130%–350% above the poverty line	34.6	39.0
130% below the poverty line	29.2	42.0

0 10 20 30 40 50

Percentage of obese aged 20 years and over

Taken from: National Center for Health Statistics (NCHS) Data Brief no. 50, December 2010.

improve the health of cities across our nation. Targeting only one aspect of the problem will not be effective in fighting the obesity epidemic, since many of its causes stem from broad social and environmental factors. Moreover, to effectively confront the disproportionate impact of obesity on low income populations, the social determinants of health—including the significant disparities that poorer people experience—must be addressed.

Working Together Is Key

Communities are the cornerstone for preventive interventions that increase the accessibility of fresh foods and physical activity, implement policies to reduce the marketing of unhealthy foods to children and adults, and help make healthy nutritional choices easier and affordable. In this regard, public-private partnerships are critical in bringing families, businesses, health care organizations, government and other stakeholders together to reverse the impact of obesity in our country.

[Cultural anthropologist] Margaret Mead once said, "Never doubt that a small group of thoughtful, committed citizens can change the world. Indeed, it is the only thing that ever has." . . . While the path to reversing the obesity epidemic in America is challenging, by working together, we can ensure a healthier future for all Americans.

SEVEN

Poverty Does Not Cause Obesity

James A. Bacon

James A. Bacon is the author of *Boomergeddon* and publisher of the blog *Bacon's Rebellion*. In the following viewpoint he rejects conventional wisdom that says poverty causes obesity. It is true that lower-income people tend to be obese, he says, but this is because of culture, not finances. Lower-income people do not buy cheap food because they are trying to maximize the amount of nutrition they can buy with their money; they buy cheap food because it tastes good and is satisfying, he says. It takes self-discipline and impulse control—which Bacon says are upper-class values—to exercise and eat healthy. Lower-income groups lack these values, which also explains why they are lower-income to begin with, he says. Bacon concludes it is not that poor people cannot afford to eat better—it is that they choose not to.

A while back, I attended the homecoming game between Collegiate and St. Christopher's, two prep schools in the Richmond, Va., area. For the most part, the parents in the football stands were well-to-do professionals, executives and business owners who could afford to pay stiff private school tuition. Midway through the game, my daughter articulated a thought that had been coalescing in my own head: "It's amazing. There aren't any fat people here."

I had quite a different impression a few years ago when, on a lark, I attended a World Wrestling Federation event, a form of entertainment favored by the working class. I was stunned. I'd never seen so many morbidly overweight people before. I felt as if I'd been teleported to the Brookhaven Clinic [a program for morbidly obese patients].

Correlation Is Not Causation

Obesity has reached epidemic proportions in the United States, surging from 13 percent of the population in 1960 to 34 percent in 2006 and contributing to epidemics of hypertension, diabetes and other chronic diseases. Treating those maladies costs an estimated $117 billion annually, half of which is financed by Medicare and Medicaid.

While everyone laments the trend, there is no consensus on what causes it. The rise of obesity coincides with the falling price of groceries over the long term and the proliferation of fast food outlets, making food more affordable and more accessible to all segments of society. But that's not a sufficient explanation. If the means to purchase more food and patronize restaurants were what made people fat, wealthy people would be the butterballs, not poor people. But the opposite is the case. It is well-documented in countries across the developed world that obesity is correlated with lower socioeconomic status.

Why would that be? One explanation blames forces beyond poor peoples' control. "Low-income and food-insecure people are especially vulnerable due to the additional risk factors associated with poverty, including limited resources, limited access to healthy and affordable foods, and limited opportunities for physical activity," asserts the Food Research and Action Center. "Households with limited resources . . . often try to stretch their food budgets by purchasing cheap, energy-dense foods that are filling—meaning that they try to maximize their calories per dollar in order to stave off hunger."

Obesity rates have soared in the United States. From 1960 to 2006 the obesity rate grew from 13 percent to 34 percent.

So, the prodigious appetite for potato chips and cheese puffs is driven by "food insecurity." Yeah, right. Here's an alternate explanation: People buy junk food because it tastes good, it gives them a brief sensation of pleasure, and they don't care about the consequences—not because they are trying to "maximize their calories per dollar."

Three economists, Charles J. Courtemanche, Garth Heutel and Patrick McAlvanah, have just written a paper, published by the National Bureau of Economic Research, exploring the influence of "time preference"—the value that people place upon present consumption versus future consumption—upon dietary choices. Some people are impatient, the authors observe. They have less impulse control. They are less willing to defer gratification.

Obesity Results from Impulsiveness

Drawing upon the 2006 National Longitudinal Survey of Youth, which includes a wealth of personal data, including Body Mass Index (BMI) as well as answers to questions regarding hypothetical time-related trade-offs, the scholars conclude: "As economic factors lower the opportunity cost of food consumption, impatient individuals gain weight while the most patient individuals do not. BMI therefore rises, but the rise is concentrated among a subset of the population."

Translation: As food has gotten more affordable over the years, some people have gotten fatter because they are more impulsive and shortsighted and prefer to eat food that gives them a quick sugar rush over healthier foods that don't.

Many lower-income people are like children from more affluent families who also suffer from impulse-control issues. My eighth-grade son, left to his own devices, would happily subsist on Cheerios, Klondike bars and macaroni and cheese. The reason he doesn't is that my wife and I strip the house bare of candy, cookies, ice cream, potato chips, Twinkies, Fritos, Cheetos, sugared soft drinks and other cheap carbs. In a grueling battle of wills, we compel him (with varying degrees of success) to work broccoli, fruit and garden salads into his diet. We subject him to lectures on how his eating habits today will affect his health and physical appearance in the far distant future—like high school.

The difference is culture. To achieve success in the United States requires a willingness to excel at school, forgo income while spending years in college, subject oneself to the strictures of the workplace and live within one's means—in sum, to stifle impulse and embrace the boring bourgeois virtues. The willingness to defer gratification is the same trait it takes to maintain disciplined eating and exercise habits over decades. That's a big reason the preppy moms and dads of Richmond have plump wallets but lean derrieres while many of the working stiffs across town are wheezing and overweight.

EIGHT

Parents of Obese Children Should Lose Custody of Them

David L. Katz

> In the following viewpoint David L. Katz suggests obese children might benefit from being taken out of their parents' custody. He considers it abusive for parents to feed their children to the point of obesity. In the same way that society would not tolerate parents giving their children cigarettes or drugs, so too should society frown upon parents who force large amounts of unhealthy food upon their children. Children are taken from their parents if they are starved; why should they not be taken away if they are overfed and/or fed junk or fatty foods, the author asks? Katz admits that any program to remove obese children from their parents' care would need to be carefully thought out. But in theory, he thinks it is appropriate to protect children from harm inflicted by their parents and considers obesity one such harm.
>
> Katz, an expert in nutrition, weight management, and chronic disease prevention, is the founding director of Yale University's Prevention Research Center.

An editorial in JAMA [the *Journal of the American Medical Association*] today [July 14, 2011,] by [Lindsey] Murtagh and [David S.] Ludwig proposes that in the case of severe childhood obesity, we should be prepared to consider state intervention. In other words, the state should potentially react to severe "overfeeding" and its consequences as it would to parents starving a child. Protecting the well-being, and life, of the child trumps the sanctity of the family.

But along with the knee-jerk opposition such a proposal evokes (in my opinion, unwarranted in this case, by the way, because Ms. Murtagh and Dr. Ludwig make a very thoughtful, nuanced argument), there is a subtle problem that may go overlooked. Namely, we condemn the outcome, but not the behavior that leads to it.

Adults are criminally liable if they give cigarettes or alcohol or illicit drugs to a child. And they are criminally liable for starving a child as well—this constitutes abuse. But our society does not view giving a child a donut or fries or soda as abusive—even if it occurs day after day. How do we sanction state intervention for a bad outcome attached to behaviors we condone every day?

Families Share Destructive Behaviors

Thinking along these lines led me back to an experience I had a few years ago, when I went to Maui to give a talk at a health conference.

What is relevant to my topic about this is the plane I took to get here. I happened to be sitting in first class, courtesy of those hosting the conference. In my row was a woman who had moved to Maui a year prior, her sister and her sister's two-year-old daughter.

I did not get to know her well, but enough to recognize that she was intelligent and warm-hearted. She was thrilled to be bringing her sister and baby niece to visit her new island home for the first time. I liked her.

There was something else I got to know about her, which required no conversation at all. Namely, she was a very large woman. Her sister, just a couple of seats away, was at least as large.

At one point during the flight, my neighbor's sister returned from the airplane lavatory and told her sister, with a chuckle in her voice, "If I get any bigger I'm not going to fit in there!" The

More than One in Six Children Are Obese

Based on a 2009–2010 survey, the Centers for Disease Control and Prevention and the National Center for Health Statistics reported that nearly 17 percent of all American children are obese. Some have suggested extreme measures—such as taking such kids out of their parents care—for dealing with the problem.

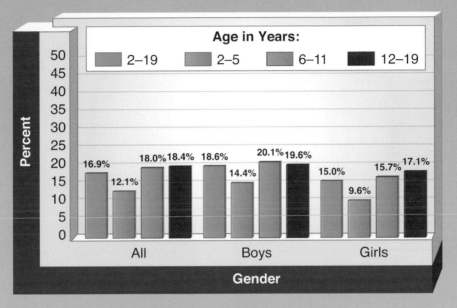

Taken from: National Center for Health Statistics (NCHS) Data Brief no. 82, January 2012.

two of them had a good laugh and exchanged quips about the need to "extend" those little toilets.

Throughout the entire flight, my neighbor (and her sister) were eating and drinking. This is hard to resist in first class, where you are constantly offered temptations. So my neighbor consumed several glasses of wine. She ate everything that was served. And she ate a box of some kind of glow-in-the-dark cheese puffs she had brought with her.

I watched my very delightful neighbor and her probably equally delightful sister share their eminently destructive behaviors with the two-year-old in their company. I have essentially no doubt that this child—still lean at age two—is destined for even more extreme obesity than her mother and aunt, and destined for the chronic diseases that ensue. In other words, I was observing a pattern of familial behavior that would destroy an innocent child's health.

Obesity Is Like Drug Use or Smoking
Imagine if two drug addicts joked in public about the health consequences of their drug use, even as they shared their drugs with a small child. Children are removed from their parents for less.

The Centers for Disease Control and Prevention says that American children will suffer more chronic disease over their lifetimes (and a greater likelihood of premature death) due to bad diet and little physical activity than they will from drugs, tobacco, and alcohol combined.

Imagine if smokers joking about their worsening emphysema put their cigarettes into the mouths of their infants. Would anyone observing this feel inclined to mind their own business?

Don't get me wrong; I am not maligning these women. Nor am I suggesting their harmful behavior was even their fault. Our society has yet to provide any clear guidelines on what is, and is not, acceptable when it comes to second-hand obesity.

That is what has to change, certainly before we sanction the state taking an obese child from a parent. Let's react to the process, not just the outcome. You don't get to decide for yourself if giving drugs or cigarettes or alcohol to small children is appropriate. Society has decided for us: It is not! Good call.

Data from the CDC [Centers for Disease Control and Prevention] indicate that children growing up in the United States today will suffer more chronic disease and premature death over their lifetimes from eating badly and lack of physical activity than from exposure to alcohol, tobacco and drugs combined. If the principle we care about is protecting children from harm, the practice should pertain to all threats comparably. At present, it does not. We are feeding our children to death.

Obesity is not the fault of its many victims, but it's no joke either. I like a good laugh as much as the next guy. But unless we start recognizing obesity for the serious threat that it is, the fate of our children will be cause for tears. And unless we take such matters into our own hands, there is the prospect in severe cases of the state taking our children into theirs.

NINE

Parents of Obese Children Should Not Lose Custody of Them

Trish Kahle

Removing obese children from their parents' care is a classist, racist solution to a complicated problem, argues Trish Kahle in the following viewpoint. She explains that throughout history, rich white people have suggested splitting up poor, minority families in misguided, elitist efforts to help them. Kahle says denying parents custody of their obese children would be no different. Obesity is a complex problem that is not merely the result of eating too much food, says Kahle. Genetics, socioeconomic status, and predatory marketing all play a role. Therefore, she claims, simply separating children from their families would not fix obesity and would place fault on the wrong party. Parents are not to blame for obesity, Kahle claims. Rather than having their children taken from them, she concludes, they need real help and better resources to improve their children's health.

Kahle is a reporter whose articles appear regularly in *Socialist Worker,* an antiestablishment publication that reports from a liberal and socialist perspective.

Ever since I first heard about the new recommendation by David Ludwig, an obesity doctor at Children's Hospital Boston, and lawyer Lindsey Murtagh, a researcher at Harvard's School of Public Health, in the *Journal of the American Medical Association* (*JAMA*) that "super obese" children should be removed from their families out of concern for their immediate health, the story has seemingly been everywhere.

While the mainstream sources raise the story as a "question" or "debate," there has been startlingly little challenging of the article's suggestion. Everyone seems unwilling to repudiate the notion which—as I'll discuss—is not only ridiculous, but also manages to target the poor for punishment, further protect and expand corporate interests, and weave racism into its ugly tapestry before the journal is even cool off the press.

Rarely in a Child's Best Interest

Even Dr. Atronette Yancey, a professor in the Department of Health Services at the UCLA [University of California, Los Angeles] School of Public Health, noted that childhood obesity stems from several factors over which parents have little control, but her conclusion was not to say removing obese children from their homes would be a bad idea, but rather that it should be a "last resort."

Even small criticisms that have been made of the proposal argue that, while it might be undesirable to remove children from their families, it would be done in the "best interests" of the child.

This argument rather disturbingly—and almost verbatim— echoes arguments that were used across the world to "justify" removing children of color from their families, and even their home countries, and placing them in the "care" of white families, a practice that continues in some areas to this day.

The logic of the proposed removals is that allowing a child to become "super obese" (whatever that means—I haven't been able to find guidelines) constitutes neglect. If one was to carry that logic through to the rest of society, what would that mean? Are "super obese" adults legally incompetent because of their

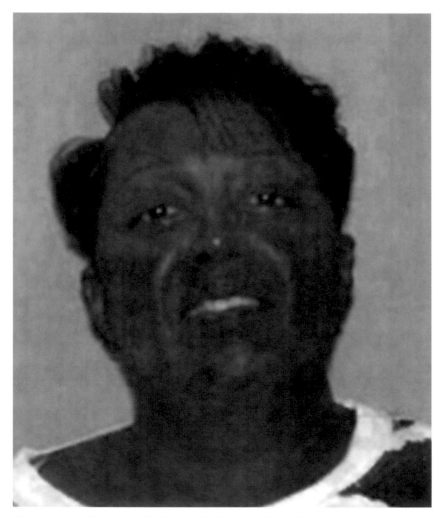

Jerri Gray (pictured) fled to Maryland with her son, who weighs 555 pounds, when she found out that her home state of North Carolina was going to charge her with medical neglect for her son's obesity.

inability to attain or maintain a healthy weight? Does not providing "super obese" prisoners with proper "treatment" constitute torture? Would elderly or dependent people who are "super obese" be considered victims of neglect as well? That none of these questions are being raised belie the fact that this policy is not even at its root driven by a desire for good health. . . .

A Racist and Classist Solution

To be clear, taking obese children away from their parents is nothing new. Long before it was put forward in *JAMA*, Alexander Draper, a Black South Carolina teen who weighed 555 pounds at the time, was taken away from his mother, Jerri Gray. When Gray found out she was going to lose custody of her son and be charged with medical neglect, she fled with her son to Maryland, where she was arrested and her son taken into protective custody to receive treatment.

The sheriff claimed that help had been offered to the family previously, but had not been accepted. It should be clear, though, that this aid did not include access to healthy food. Gray explained that programs had been inaccessible or ineffective, and that she had sought help for her son and not received it.

She cited two major obstacles to providing her son with a healthy diet: low wages and long, odd hours. Gray didn't have the money to purchase healthier food options, and her work hours meant that she didn't have time to cook for her son. Her financial and employment situations dictated that most of his meals were high-calorie, high-fat fast food that had otherwise low nutritional content.

This was not "bad decision-making" on her part, though the media certainly portrayed it that way. Gray knew that fast food was not the healthiest option for her son. Instead, it was the inevitable outcome of a reality with restricted food choices—a reality the wealthy never have to face.

Parents Need Help, Money, and Time

The story of Alexander Draper and Jerri Gray is typical. Every single case I was able to find of an obese child being removed from his/her family involved a Black family and usually a single mother who cited long hours and low wages as the chief obstacle to providing a healthy diet to her family.

Certainly, there are white and affluent children who are obese. Class is just one cause of obesity, but a very large one. Obesity in affluent children is more likely to stem from an eating disorder rather than inability to access healthy foods and exercise facilities.

Under capitalism, health is something we buy, not something to which we are entitled as a fundamental human right. This means that regardless of whether wealthy children are obese, they will not be targeted if this program is implemented based on the *JAMA* recommendations. Their families could afford expensive medical care that would preclude being taken into "protective custody."

No, it is the poor that will be the target of any policy instituted based on these recommendations. And despite the fact that parents have few, if any, healthy options available on a low-income budget, parents are the ones being blamed for "poor choices."

A better focus would be the poor ethical choices of marketing and corporate agriculture. While these choices fit in marvelously with the morals of capitalism, they grate viciously against common human decency.

Essentially, corporate agriculture has manufactured chemicals out of food and non-food items that will sustain working-class life (in the most basic sense) with no concern for the long-term health effects—whether it be obesity or cancer. Then, the marketing industry has convinced us that this "stuff" is actually "food." Think "Soylent Green" [a 1973 film in which people were fed food processed from dead human bodies], only with less cannibalism.

And consider this: it is cheaper to buy soda, with high-fructose corn syrup as one of its main ingredients, than it is to buy bottled water (and the poorer you are, the less likely your tap water is safe to drink). In addition, since so many working-class people are overworked, overstressed and in a constant state of fatigue, many use the sodas with sugars and caffeine to help them "get through the day"—i.e., keep their jobs.

The Poor Have Fewer Options

While the wealthy among us might be able to stroll through Trader Joe's, Whole Foods and Earthfare [specialty grocery stores], and have their choice of good fruits and vegetables, and whole grain, pesticide-free foods, that's not an option available to most of us. After all, the $4 you might spend on a tomato in such a store will buy a week's worth of boxed macaroni and cheese or ramen noodles. The "choice" of what food to buy is about as meaningful as the right to quit your job if you don't like your boss. In other words, not a choice at all.

However, the rhetorical construction of this choice serves the ruling class extraordinarily well. It fits the ideological construction of working-class people as stupid and unfit to make important choices, a construction that is necessary to the maintenance of capitalism as a system. After all, they argue, if they can't even make healthy eating decisions, how can they possibly run society?

The construction of choice also helps maintain the illusion that the super-rich are somehow biologically superior to us. They

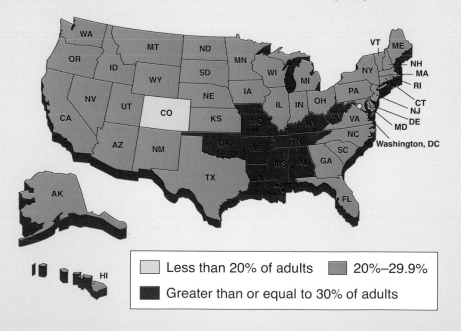

Obesity: An American Problem

Nearly every state is getting fatter. In 2009 nine states had obesity rates of 30 percent or more compared with no states in 2000. Because obesity is so widespread, some argue removing obese children from their parents' care is an overly simplistic solution to a complex problem.

Less than 20% of adults   20%–29.9%

Greater than or equal to 30% of adults

Taken from: CDC Vital Signs, August 2010.

maintain—whether explicitly or implicitly—that they are the Darwinian champions [i.e., by virtue of evolution] of society, neglecting of course their personal pools, tennis courts, trainers, and all-natural, organic stocked pantry. (Working-class people are far less likely to have a safe place to exercise, access to a pool, etc.) When necessary, the rich can afford medications and weight-loss surgery.

Discrimination at Its Worst

But even in the working class, all people aren't targeted equally. Black families seem to be the favored target for discrimination for many of the classic racist reasons. (Name one, they all fit.) Whether it's the "good-ol'-white-folks" trying to "help" Black families by breaking them up, or whether it's claiming that the (white) doctors "know better," this program will surely go down in the long history of racism in this country if it is implemented.

Every online news story discussing these proposed guidelines featured Black children in the photos, not too subtly suggesting that they would be the primary targets of such a program because their parents "don't care" and won't "pull their acts together" to save the children. I have not seen the issue of racism raised once by any commentator anywhere even though it is already embedded into this tactic of removal (not to mention the connection one might make to the way families were split up during slavery). Disgusting.

Health—*real health*, not a definition of health narrowly based on body shape or size—is a huge issue in working-class communities, but parents are not the problem and removing kids from their families isn't the solution.

TEN

Taxing Junk Food and Soda Ingredients Can Reduce Obesity

David Lazarus

In the following viewpoint David Lazarus explains why
he thinks junk food, soda, and other unhealthy foods
should be taxed. Because such foods are toxic to the
human body, Lazarus claims, he thinks they should be
treated like alcohol or tobacco. These substances are
legal to consume, but users must pay a tax to enjoy them,
he points out; the money raised by such taxes goes to
good causes, such as antismoking campaigns, which in
turn help reduce smoking. Lazarus thinks the problem
of obesity—which costs Americans billions in health
care and reduces their quality of life—should be tackled
in the same way. Putting a tax of as little as one penny
per ounce on soda and other sugary drinks could raise
billions of dollars, which could be spent funding physical
fitness programs, healthy eating initiatives, and other
important antiobesity programs, the author asserts, con-
cluding that a modest tax on soda and other junk food
is a reasonable way to fight obesity.

Lazarus is a columnist for the *Los Angeles Times*.

L et's call it what it is: a sin tax.
    A California lawmaker is targeting the obesity epidemic with a tax that would slap a penny-an-ounce levy on drinks sweetened with sugar or corn syrup.

The food industry, not surprisingly, has squared off against the idea, arguing that the tax bill is a punitive assault on personal choice.

"The government doesn't have the right to social engineer," said J. Justin Wilson, senior research analyst at the industry-backed Center for Consumer Freedom. "It doesn't have a right to protect us from ourselves."

No? The food folk are correct that this is a way of punishing people for unhealthy behavior. But they're wrong when they say the government has no role to play in prodding people to do better.

Treat Junk Food Like Alcohol and Tobacco

The other prominent sin taxes out there, for tobacco and alcohol, raise money for health and education programs, and that's a good thing. But their main purpose is to make these products more expensive and thus less attractive to potential users.

Considering that about two-thirds of American adults and a third of our kids are now overweight or obese, it seems more than reasonable to extend the same thinking to sugary drinks, which researchers say are a key contributor to the obesity epidemic.

That said, soda isn't the sole culprit. If we're serious about shedding all those excess pounds, it'll take more than just making Coke and Pepsi more expensive. More on that in a moment.

First, let's take a closer look at AB 669, the legislation introduced last week [in February 2011] by [California] Assemblyman William Monning (D-Carmel). He serves as chairman of the Assembly Health Committee.

The bill would levy an excise tax of 1 cent per ounce on any beverage with caloric sweeteners such as sugar and high-fructose corn syrup. These beverages include sodas, energy drinks and sports drinks.

The estimated $1.7 billion raised by the tax annually would be dedicated exclusively to funding physical fitness and childhood obesity programs statewide that are now facing cuts because of California's ongoing budget woes.

The money would go toward activities and gear at schools and nonprofit organizations intended to get kids off their keisters—sports, games, play equipment. It would go toward providing

Sugar Is so Dangerous, It Should Be Taxed

The authors of a 2012 study published in the journal *Nature*, argue sugar causes many of the same problems as alcohol when consumed in large amounts. For this reason, they think it should be taxed.

Chronic ethanol (alcohol) exposure	Chronic fructose exposure
Hematologic disorders	
Electrolyte abnormalities	
Hypertension	Hypertension (uric acid)
Cardiac dilatation	
Cardiomyopathy	Myocardial infarction (dyslipidemia, insulin resistance)
Dyslipidemia	Dyslipidemia (de novo lipogenesis)
Pancreatitis	Pancreatitis (hypertriglyceridemia)
Obesity (insulin resistance)	Obesity (insulin resistance)
Malnutrition	Malnutrition (obesity)
Hepatic dysfunction (alcoholic steatohepatitis)	Hepatic dysfunction (non-alcoholic steatohepatitis)
Fetal alcohol syndrome	
Addiction	Habituation, if not addiction

Taken from: Robert H. Lustig, Laura A. Schmidt, and Claire D. Brindas. "The Toxic Truth About Sugar." *Nature*, vol. 482, February 2, 2012, p. 28.

more-healthful lunch choices and efforts to educate kids about eating right.

A Public Response to a Public Problem

That won't do the whole job, of course. Parents also have some heavy lifting to do by making smarter choices at the grocery store and drive-through window. But it's better than doing nothing as kids scarf junk food and plop in front of the TV.

"These beverages have zero nutritional value, and the advertising that targets children is massive," Monning told me.

He rejected the food industry's claim that government has no role to play in influencing people's behavior.

"What we're trying to respond to is the social engineering that corporate advertising does every day," Monning said. "That's the real social engineering."

He said the impact of beverage marketing is most profound in lower-income and minority communities, where studies show that soda is frequently consumed on a daily basis and as a routine part of meals.

One recent study found that adult obesity rates for blacks and Latinos is higher than for whites in nearly every state.

The adult obesity rate for blacks is at least 30% in 43 states and the District of Columbia, according to the Trust for America's Health and the Robert Wood Johnson Foundation. The adult obesity rate for Latinos is at least 30% in 19 states. Only one state, West Virginia, has an adult obesity rate for whites greater than 30%.

"This is a public health response to a public health epidemic," Monning said of his bill.

Wilson of the Center for Consumer Freedom, which is funded primarily by the food industry, countered that people have a right to drink unhealthful beverages if that's their choice. "Soda is not a problem," he said. "It's a simple pleasure."

The real problem, Wilson said, is "overconsumption of calories," and soda accounts for less than 10% of the average person's daily calorie intake.

That may be true, responded Harold Goldstein, executive director of the California Center for Public Health Advocacy, but the calories from soda constitute a significant portion of the extra, unneeded amount that makes people fat.

California's AB 669 would have taxed any beverage containing caloric sweeteners like sugar and high-fructose corn syrup.

A 2009 report by UC [University of California] Berkeley's Center for Weight and Health found that from the 1970s to 2000, the average person's daily food consumption increased by 300 calories. Of that amount, "the increase in calorie consumption from sweetened beverages is equivalent to 43% of the total increase in calorie consumption," the report found.

"It's the equivalent of drinking a piece of chocolate cake any time you're thirsty," Goldstein said.

So making soda more expensive, and devoting the additional revenue to anti-obesity efforts, makes a lot of sense both socially and economically—just as we've seen for tobacco and alcohol. But it's not the whole answer.

The food industry and health advocates agree that what's needed is significant change in people's behavior. Put simply, we need to eat less and exercise more.

Taxes Can Be a Good Start

Personal responsibility is important. But if that alone were sufficient to keep us fit and trim, we wouldn't be a nation of porkers and porkers-in-waiting.

That's why I'd take Monning's soda tax and expand it to fast food—say, a penny for every 500 calories served.

A 540-calorie Big Mac at McDonald's would net an extra penny. So would a 500-calorie large order of fries. A 32-ounce chocolate Triple Thick Shake, at 1,160 calories, would bring in two cents.

Factor in all the other stuff bought every day at all fast-food chains, and you can see we'd be talking about some serious money. That money in turn would be used for creation of bike paths, basketball courts and other fitness-related resources.

It could also be used to help subsidize gym memberships (which health insurers should do as well, if they really want to cut their long-term costs).

The food industry is right: A soda tax won't solve the obesity epidemic. Sin taxes in general aren't going to make problems go away.

But they're a good place to start.

ELEVEN

Junk Food and Soda Should Not Be Taxed

Andrew P. Morriss

Imposing "fat taxes" on products such as junk food and soda is an inappropriate way to address the obesity problem, argues Andrew P. Morriss in the following viewpoint. Morriss takes issue with any kind of tax that punishes people for enjoying a product. Being able to eat and drink what one wants is part and parcel of being an American, and he thinks taxes that aim to curb those pleasures violate people's freedom. In addition, Morriss says that money raised from so-called sin taxes—such as taxes on alcohol or tobacco—is often wasted. Proponents of such taxes envision the billions raised to go toward health programs, fitness centers, and other utopian fixtures, but in reality, says Morriss, the money will be misspent. A very tiny percentage of money raised by smoking taxes has gone toward antismoking programs, for example, and Morriss expects the same to be true for taxes on food. For these reasons and more, he opposes taxes on junk food, soda, sugar, and other obesity-causing foods.

Morriss teaches law and business at the University of Alabama.

Proponents of an American Nanny State [a government perceived as controlling its citizens' welfare] have a plan to improve your health: tax sugar and "junk" food so you will eat less of it. Subsidies for broccoli and beets are close behind. These plans for bureaucrats and politicians to remake your diet are bad news for four reasons.

Taxes Infringe on Freedom

First, it is no one's business but yours what you eat. The freedom to eat a slice of apple pie might not sound quite as stirring as freedom of speech, but the ability to choose how to live our lives is the most fundamental freedom. What you eat is no one's business but yours.

Second, even if the government has a role to play in guiding our dietary choices, efforts at restructuring Americans' lives via the tax code are fundamentally flawed.

This strategy has given us a tax system of unimaginable complexity: the Internal Revenue Code is almost 10 million words long, and if you stacked IRS [Internal Revenue Service] regulations into a pile they'd be more than a foot tall. The leading publication for tax professionals takes up nine feet of shelf space. And that doesn't count the tens of thousands of pages of laws and regulations concerning sales, use, property, excise, and other taxes levied by all layers of government.

Taxes need to be simple and easy to administer. As tax laws get fatter, they clog our economic arteries and stifle economic growth. Trying to fine tune Americans' diets via a "junk food" tax will further fatten the tax laws, and the wallets of accountants and tax lawyers. If there are any Americans unaware that sugar and potato chips are fattening—despite our $35 billion per year diet industry—we don't need a tax to enlighten them, just some public service announcements.

Third, the government's record on dietary control is problematic. The federal government has been involved in the sugar market since the War of 1812. Nanny Staters promise that this time they'll get things right but if they haven't managed to do so in 200 years, why should we believe them now?

Single 2-Liter Bottle
Consumer Cost + Tax $1.21
The Mayor's Tax $1.35
Sales Tax $ .11

New Price $2.67

Case of 12 oz Cans
Dealer Cost $ 6.50
The Mayor's Tax $ 5.76

New Price $12.26

SAY NO
TO THE BEVERAGE TAX

SAY NO
TO THE BEVERAGE TAX

SAY NO
TO THE BEVERAGE TAX

SAY NO
TO THE BEVERAGE TA

Philadelphians protest mayor Michael Nutter's proposed tax on nondiet sodas and other sugary drinks sold in the city.

The details of official rules are written in back rooms in Congress and government agencies. When those details are drafted, those best able to influence the results are the lawyers and lobbyists for special interest groups.

For sugar, that's the manufacturers of high fructose corn syrup and the 17 domestic sugar cane producers who reap millions of dollars annually under our current agricultural subsidies and sugar tariffs—not you and me.

The Money Will Be Wasted

Finally, the Nanny State brigade promises to spend the extra tax money on subsidies for "healthy" foods and lifestyles. *New York Times* columnist Matt Bittman enthuses about money for "gyms, pools, jogging and bike trails," "Meals on Wheels" for the elderly, "Head Start" programs for children, and "supermarkets and farmers' markets."

A 2012 poll conducted by Google Consumer Surveys found that nearly three in four Americans oppose a tax on fatty or sweet foods.

Question: To encourage good eating and to fund health care, would you support a tax on high-fat and high-sugar foods?

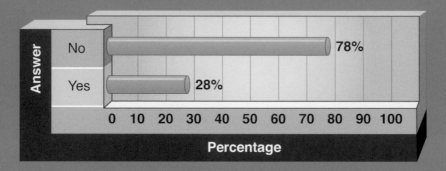

Taken from: David Maris. "Is a Fat Tax in America's Future?" *Forbes*, April 19, 2012. Conducted by Google Consumer Surveys, April 6–13, 2012 and based on 1,182 online responses.

If we examine the government's record in spending the billions of dollars from state governments' lawsuits against tobacco companies, we can see that this is pure fantasy.

Remember when the states settled their lawsuits against the tobacco companies in 1998? The settlements produced billions in new state revenues from higher cigarette prices.

States promised to spend vast sums on anti-smoking programs. The reality is different. The Campaign for Tobacco-Free Kids tracks state tobacco prevention spending and tobacco revenues and found that over the first ten years of the settlement, states spent just 3.2 percent of the money on tobacco prevention and cessation programs.

Nanny Staters promise the sun, moon and stars to get new taxes on the books, but deliver little else.

TWELVE

Healthier School Lunches Can Reduce Obesity

Mary Sanchez

> In the following viewpoint Mary Sanchez argues that making school lunches healthier can help curb child obesity. Sanchez explains that school lunch is an important meal for children—they receive more than a third of their total daily calories at school. Yet too often, says Sanchez, school lunches are not nutritious. Meals are designed by politicians and lobbyists (people who advocate for their state's or industry's interests, such as the corn, sugar, or wheat industry), not nutritionists. In Sanchez's opinion, school lunches should be designed not on the basis of industry preferences but on what is best for children. She concludes that school lunch periods offer a much-needed opportunity to both curb child obesity and help students become better learners.
>
> Sanchez is a columnist for the *Kansas City Star*, a daily Missouri newspaper.

See if you can score higher on this pop quiz than members of the U.S. Congress:

How much tomato paste must one slather onto a slice of pizza for it to qualify as a nutritionally adequate serving of vegetables for low-income schoolchildren?

A quarter cup? A half cup? Two tablespoons?

It's a trick question. A tomato is actually a fruit. But let's leave aside the horticultural definition and talk about how Congress failed the quiz. It chose 2 tablespoons, blocking sorely needed nutritional upgrades to the $11 billion federal school lunch programs. It did so because members' brains (and quite possibly their bellies) are controlled by lobbyists.

Laughable Nutritional Standards

Two tablespoons is about the amount of paste commonly found on the cardboard slices that pose as pizza in far too many school cafeterias. That amount will continue to qualify as a vegetable serving. Did I mention the frozen food lobby?

Let's move on to another question. How many servings of potatoes, aka french fries, is it wise to serve to children before their diet becomes too laden with starch? Congress' answer? An unlimited number!

And let's not even go into the question of whether it is wise, as was suggested by the Department of Agriculture, that school lunches require at least half of the breads served each week be from whole grains. Congress pleaded ignorance, claiming it needed a better definition on what exactly is a whole grain.

In a healthier world, Congress should have argued for a different option. In January [2011], the U.S. Department of Agriculture [USDA] issued new guidelines for school lunches, as mandated by a 2004 act of Congress. The new rules called for limiting starchy vegetables, reducing sodium and raising the amount of tomato sauce that could be considered a vegetable serving, among other changes. The frozen pizza and french fry lobby was not pleased. According to *The New York Times*, the food industry spent $5.6 million lobbying against the new rules.

Clearly, all of [First Lady] Michelle Obama's digging in the White House garden, among other attempts to steer the nation's children toward fresh fruits and vegetables, just got clobbered. If anyone needs more evidence that the U.S. Congress is working on behalf of lobbyists, rather than in the best interests of the nation, this charade is it.

The nutritional guidelines for the National School Lunch Program hadn't been updated in 15 years. During that time, obesity rates among children skyrocketed. One-third of American children are either overweight or obese, with rates of diabetes and other health-related issues also showing dangerous increases. Children receive about 40 percent of their daily calories from school lunches, so there is a connection.

The prepared foods and big agriculture industries were not the only ones pushing back against the new USDA rules. School

The Government Should Play a Role

The majority of Americans think the government should play a significant role in reducing obesity among children. This could include mandating that school lunches feature healthier, fresher ingredients.

Question: "Do you think the government should or should not play a significant role in reducing obesity among children?"

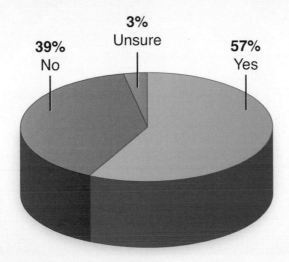

39%
No

3%
Unsure

57%
Yes

Taken from: Pew Research Center, February 22–March 1, 2011.

officials, especially in big cities, were concerned about how the changes might affect their ability to feed needy students.

Reduced-cost and free lunch menus provide meals for 31 million children each school year. The federal government pays schools a maximum of $2.94 for each lunch served. The changes

Healthy school lunches have been found to reduce obesity in teens.

were expected to increase the costs of the school lunches by 14 cents—not a trifling amount when added up. School officials also wanted more flexibility, especially on issues such as the number of starches that would be allowed. For instance, baked potatoes are a nutritionally sound choice.

And, predictably, conservative ideologues added their anti-government bromides to the debate, lamenting the USDA rules' incursion on "choice."

Healthy Children Learn Better

Maybe if Congress had worked more to find middle ground with the American Association of School Administrators, the lawmakers might have found more leverage and courage to push back on the food lobbyists. They might even have shifted attitudes in the food industry about which food offerings can be profitable in cafeterias.

The connections between obesity and poverty and health problems are undeniable, and ignoring school lunch nutrition just makes them more expensive for the taxpayer. So, to the outcry that the federal government shouldn't be telling schools what to serve in the cafeteria, here's a parental reply: As long as we're paying the bills for these programs, you'll serve what we tell you to!

A strong argument can be made that healthier children are more ready to learn. Healthy children also have fewer school absences, are more engaged in their studies and quite possibly will behave better. Now, what educator would work against that outcome?

As any parent can attest, getting children to upgrade their food habits can be difficult. Temper tantrums, hiding the peas under the knife, tossing the unwanted fresh fruit into the trash, or choosing the higher calorie strawberry and chocolate milk are real issues.

Getting Congress to act the adult, to vote in the best interests of children, shouldn't be an even more daunting task.

THIRTEEN

Healthier School Lunches Will Not Reduce Obesity

Trevor Butterworth

In the following viewpoint Trevor Butterworth explains why making school lunches healthier will have no impact on obesity. He argues that for kids, lunchtime is largely social—they use the time to hang out with their friends and eat what tastes good or is convenient. When schools pour money into upgrading their lunch menus with nutritionally sound dishes, most students are not interested. They either do not like such food and will not eat it, says Butterworth, or they rebel against school authorities for telling them what they should eat. Either way, the food—which is expensive and takes money away from other school programs, such as physical education—ends up getting thrown out. For these reasons, Butterworth thinks the only result of making school lunches healthier will be lots of wasted food and money.

Butterworth is a journalist and columnist whose articles have appeared in *Newsweek,* the *Wall Street Journal,* and the Daily, an online news site.

As acronyms go, HHFKA sounds as if it might be a covert insult in the jargon of government bureaucracy, a cluster of ill-chosen letters begging for contraction. It actually stands for the "Healthy, Hunger-Free Kids Act," which was signed into law in 2010 by President [Barack] Obama, and which returned to the news recently when the U.S. Department of Agriculture [USDA] announced new nutritional rules on the food served in schools. More fruits and veggies! Less fat and sodium! Hurrah!

And indeed, there was much hurrahing in the media, in part because news organizations went to the same two activist groups for comment. One was the Center for Science in the Public Interest, which, to be fair, offered only muted applause, because the USDA had failed to limit the amount of fries that could be served with that delicious pile of kale. The other? The

Cafeteria workers prepare healthy foods for students at a New York school. Critics say the kids do not like the healthy foods, and throw the food away.

Environmental Working Group, a green advocacy group that has only just entered the field of nutrition, but which, nevertheless, proclaimed that the changes would save billions of dollars in health-care costs in the future.

Food Preferences Are Personal and Individual

Now, I have nothing against more veggies. As a child, I was fed from our vegetable garden. But even back in the 1970s, my mother was quickly informed by her peers that it was nothing short of miraculous that I, at 5, would willingly eat an entire head of cabbage (this was Ireland, so having it boiled to death might have helped with digestion). By way of contrast, the kid next door wouldn't eat vegetables at all.

So the question is not whether tinkering with school menu options will produce better food—of course it will. The question is better for whom? The adults, activists, doctors and bureaucrats who want to see childhood obesity reversed—or the kids who arrive at school, their taste buds calibrated by the food choices made by their parents?

Unfortunately, there is reason to worry that the latest HHFKA initiative may do little more than create a lot of vegetable waste. The evidence comes from Britain, which implemented similar but even more stringent nutritional rules after celebrity chef Jamie Oliver exposed the ugly world of school canteen food in 2005. Naturally, all the adults thought the new menus, designed by Oliver, were worth the extra cost. To their eyes, the food looked marvelous, appetizing, nutritious—and therefore compelling. But what did the kids think?

In a remarkable piece of survey research, public health experts at Oxford University went out into schools to get the consumer perspective just as the new nutritional rules were coming into effect. Far from being drones for Big Food, it turns out, the kids were well aware of the differences between healthy and unhealthy diets. However, here's the problem: Health was not the driving force in deciding what to eat. Instead, lunch breaks were valued as time to socialize with their peers, which meant that vending

machine food was the most efficient way of maximizing this social time. You didn't have to line up—and you weren't restricted to eating in an ugly canteen (which was another complaint).

Even more astonishing, the kids turned out to be instinctively libertarian: As the study notes, they were "often vociferous in defending their supposed 'rights'"—and "frustrated with the government for imposing 'unfair' and 'harsh' policies on their freedom." As one grade-school kid put it to the Oxford researchers, "We decide what we eat. It's not their [the government's] choice. It's our freedom of eating."

Healthy Lunches Get Wasted

And so it came to pass that kids rebelled against the new government menus by bringing their own food to school; and when the schools tried to regulate that according to the new nutritional guidelines, the kids simply went off campus to buy food from shops and cafes. Predictably, this led some adults to argue that these establishments should be outlawed—to which the British health secretary said, in effect, where does this end? It certainly doesn't seem to end in weight loss. "The fruit and veg campaign in the U.K. [United Kingdom] has been very expensive and had no impact on obesity," said Professor Thomas Sanders, professor of nutrition and dietetics at King's College London. "There is high awareness of the five [servings] a day campaign and it is the overweight and obese who are most likely to report eating five a day!"

The problem with tackling obesity in schools through nutrition is that students spend a lot of time in school sitting around. And then they spend a lot of time at home sitting around, thanks to computers, video games and television. But what has been steadily subjected to school budget cutting even as the nutrition budget is now set to increase by $3.2 billion? Physical education and sports.

FOURTEEN

Obesity Can Be Prevented by Making Healthy Foods Cheaper

Mattea Kramer

The cost of healthy foods needs to come down in order for low-income families to afford them, argues Mattea Kramer in the following viewpoint. Kramer says the link between obesity and poverty is real and proven—healthy foods simply cost too much for poor families to buy. The poor are therefore more likely to be overweight and obese than people who can afford to pay higher prices for fresh fruits and vegetables, whole grains, lean meats, and other pricey items. Kramer thinks the government needs to subsidize the costs of such foods, which means contributing money to their production so their in-store cost can be lower. Kramer suggests the government divert funds away from ineffective programs, which would free up millions of dollars that could be put toward lowering the cost of healthy food.

Kramer is a senior research analyst at the National Priorities Project, where she specializes in food policy, public health, and political campaigns.

End childhood obesity within a generation—this is the goal of first lady Michelle Obama's Let's Move initiative. Mrs. Obama's campaign focuses on sedentary children and lots of unhealthy snacking as the drivers of childhood obesity. In the national dialogue on obesity among adults, the discussion isn't hugely different: Overweight Americans lack the self-control to pursue a healthier lifestyle, while certain agricultural subsidies make the unhealthiest foods the cheapest. But the obesity crisis is a lot more complicated than that.

Many Poor Families Cannot Eat Well

It turns out that the kind of diet that complies with the Department of Agriculture's [USDA's] official dietary guidelines is unaffordable for many Americans.

A researcher at the University of Washington found that an income level that qualifies a family for food stamp assistance makes it nearly impossible to put healthy and balanced meals on the table. Though food stamp benefits are calculated to allow families to buy the lowest-cost foods that are still nutritious, the USDA's own research shows that food prices vary widely across the country. That means if you live in a region with high prices (such as the Northeast), it may be unaffordable for you to feed your family healthy meals.

Obesity isn't entirely—or even primarily—a question of willpower, but has a lot to do with socioeconomic status. Federal policy should address this by making healthy foods cheaper.

Journalists have popularized a link between cheap junk food and subsidies to the corn industry. But this isn't the reason why junk food is cheaper than fresh fruits and vegetables. Even with no subsidies for corn production, fresh produce is more expensive because it has a short shelf life. It has to be picked, shipped, stocked, purchased, and eaten quickly to prevent spoilage. Rolling back commodity supports won't make healthier options the cheapest. The solution, as proposed by former US Assistant Attorney General Robert Raben, is subsidies for fruits and vegetables.

Price sends a strong signal, especially for those on a thin budget. In Massachusetts, for example, there are innovative programs at work to make nutritious foods cheaper for those who can least afford them. Many farmers' markets not only accept food stamp benefits, but they also use public and donated funds to double the

A student buys a lunch of fruits and vegetables at a school cafeteria. Government subsidies could make the costs of healthful foods like these more accessible to the poor.

value of food stamps when they're used at farmers' markets—so they go twice as far toward buying fruits and veggies.

The Massachusetts Department of Agriculture estimates that this matching program and other outreach efforts increased farmers' market sales to food stamp recipients by 300 percent. Lawmakers in Washington should make federal funds available to support this innovation.

Money Should Be Spent Subsidizing Healthy Foods

Of course, members of Congress have pledged to slash, not grow, government spending this year, so a new subsidy for fruits and vegetables is a nonstarter. But there are ways to pay for it without spilling more red ink.

The Dollar Menu

One dollar buys varying amounts of food and calories. For example, a dollar can buy four eggs (360 calories), less than half a head of lettuce (16.5 calories), or a whole McDonald's hamburger (390 calories). In this way, unhealthy food can be much cheaper than healthy food, and one of the reasons advocates say the price of healthy food must come down if the United States is to curb obesity.

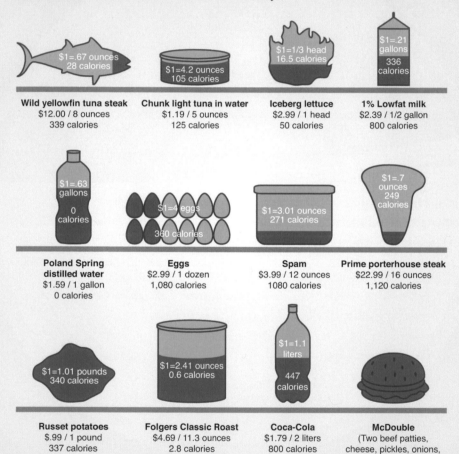

Wild yellowfin tuna steak
$12.00 / 8 ounces
339 calories

$1=.67 ounces
28 calories

Chunk light tuna in water
$1.19 / 5 ounces
125 calories

$1=4.2 ounces
105 calories

Iceberg lettuce
$2.99 / 1 head
50 calories

$1=1/3 head
16.5 calories

1% Lowfat milk
$2.39 / 1/2 gallon
800 calories

$1=.21 gallons
336 calories

Poland Spring distilled water
$1.59 / 1 gallon
0 calories

$1=.63 gallons
0 calories

Eggs
$2.99 / 1 dozen
1,080 calories

$1=4 eggs
360 calories

Spam
$3.99 / 12 ounces
1080 calories

$1=3.01 ounces
271 calories

Prime porterhouse steak
$22.99 / 16 ounces
1,120 calories

$1=.7 ounces
249 calories

Russet potatoes
$.99 / 1 pound
337 calories

$1=1.01 pounds
340 calories

Folgers Classic Roast
$4.69 / 11.3 ounces
2.8 calories

$1=2.41 ounces
0.6 calories

Coca-Cola
$1.79 / 2 liters
800 calories

$1=1.1 liters
447 calories

McDouble
(Two beef patties, cheese, pickles, onions, ketchup, mustard)
$1.00
390 calories

Taken from: Peter Smith. "How Much—Could You Eat on a Dollar?" *Good*, June 30, 2011; and *Latham's Quarterly*.

A child nutrition bill that was passed in October [2011] allocated $375 million for state programs dedicated to preventing obesity and educating low-income Americans about healthy eating. That's a lot of money to spend printing nutrition pamphlets, which are an unproven means of promoting health.

Congress should shift half of the funds to direct nutrition support, to double food stamp benefits when they're used to buy healthy items at farmers' markets. This wouldn't cost taxpayers another penny, but it would improve the effectiveness of money already in the pipeline.

Such changes are authorized in the farm bill, which is written on a four-year cycle. Discussions over the 2012 farm bill are already under way. Now is our chance to make real strides toward improving health and tackling obesity. Let's not miss it.

FIFTEEN

Healthy Food Is Cheap Enough but Americans Do Not Choose It

Mark Bittman

In the following viewpoint Mark Bittman challenges the notion that junk and fast food are cheaper than fresh foods and thus obese poor people cannot afford to lose weight by eating healthier. This may be true of gourmet organic foods, he says, but not of regular, healthy ingredients. Bittman argues that a home-cooked meal made from simple, affordable ingredients—such as chicken and vegetables, or rice and beans—is less expensive per person than fast food and much healthier. Bittman says people turn to fast food for convenience; some may even become addicted to the taste. Recognizing that choice— more than finances—contributes to obesity is important, says Bittman. If the United States wants to genuinely reduce obesity, it must attack the cultural values that lead people to view cooking as work and fast food as indulgent.

Bittman is a food columnist for the *New York Times*.

The "fact" that junk food is cheaper than real food has become a reflexive part of how we explain why so many Americans are overweight, particularly those with lower incomes. I frequently read confident statements like, "when a bag of chips is cheaper than a head of broccoli . . ." or "it's more affordable to feed a family of four at McDonald's than to cook a healthy meal for them at home."

This is just plain wrong. In fact it isn't cheaper to eat highly processed food: a typical order for a family of four—for example, two Big Macs, a cheeseburger, six chicken McNuggets, two medium and two small fries, and two medium and two small sodas—costs, at the McDonald's a hundred steps from where I write, about $28. (Judicious ordering of "Happy Meals" can reduce that to about $23—and you get a few apple slices in addition to the fries!)

In general, despite extensive government subsidies, hyperprocessed food remains more expensive than food cooked at home. You can serve a roasted chicken with vegetables along with a simple salad and milk for about $14, and feed four or even six people. If that's too much money, substitute a meal of rice and canned beans with bacon, green peppers and onions; it's easily enough for four people and costs about $9. (Omitting the bacon, using dried beans, which are also lower in sodium, or substituting carrots for the peppers reduces the price further, of course.)

Another argument runs that junk food is cheaper when measured by the calorie, and that this makes fast food essential for the poor because they need cheap calories. But given that half of the people in this country (and a higher percentage of poor people) consume too many calories rather than too few, measuring food's value by the calorie makes as much sense as measuring a drink's value by its alcohol content. (Why not drink 95 percent neutral grain spirit, the cheapest way to get drunk?)

Different Kinds of Calories Matter

Besides, that argument, even if we all needed to gain weight, is not always true. A meal of real food cooked at home can easily contain more calories, most of them of the "healthy" variety. (Olive oil accounts for many of the calories in the roast chicken meal, for example.) In comparing prices of real food and junk food, I used supermarket ingredients, not the pricier organic or local food that many people would consider ideal. But food choices are not black and white; the alternative to fast food is not necessarily organic food, any more than the alternative to soda is Bordeaux [French wine].

The alternative to soda is water, and the alternative to junk food is not grass-fed beef and greens from a trendy farmers' market, but anything other than junk food: rice, grains, pasta, beans, fresh vegetables, canned vegetables, frozen vegetables, meat, fish, poultry, dairy products, bread, peanut butter, a thousand other things cooked at home—in almost every case a far superior alternative.

"Anything that you do that's not fast food is terrific; cooking once a week is far better than not cooking at all," says Marion Nestle, professor of food studies at New York University and author of *What to Eat*. "It's the same argument as exercise: more is better than less and some is a lot better than none."

The fact is that most people can afford real food. Even the nearly 50 million Americans who are enrolled in the Supplemental Nutrition Assistance Program (formerly known as food stamps) receive about $5 per person per day, which is far from ideal but enough to survive. So we have to assume that money alone doesn't guide decisions about what to eat. There are, of course, the so-called food deserts, places where it's hard to find food: the Department of Agriculture says that more than two million Americans in low-income rural areas live 10 miles or more from a supermarket, and more than five million households without access to cars live more than a half mile from a supermarket.

Still, 93 percent of those with limited access to supermarkets do have access to vehicles, though it takes them 20 more minutes to travel to the store than the national average. And after a long day of work at one or even two jobs, 20 extra minutes—plus cooking time—must seem like an eternity.

Taking the long route to putting food on the table may not be easy, but for almost all Americans it remains a choice, and if you can drive to McDonald's you can drive to Safeway [a supermarket]. It's cooking that's the real challenge. (The real challenge is not "I'm too busy to cook." In 2010 the average American,

A 2009 study by the Scripps Research Institute found that overconsumption of fast foods triggers addiction-like responses in the brain, which means that one must eat more and more fast food to be satisfied.

regardless of weekly earnings, watched no less than an hour and a half of television per day. The time is there.)

We Need to Think Beyond Convenience

The core problem is that cooking is defined as work, and fast food is both a pleasure and a crutch. "People really are stressed out with all that they have to do, and they don't want to cook,"

Fast Food Is Not so Cheap

A *New York Times* report found it is less expensive to make a home-cooked meal using reasonably good quality ingredients than it is to buy fast food. Such meals were also much healthier.

Comparison Shopping:

McDonald's for Four
$27.89

- 2 Big Macs
- 1 cheeseburger
- 1 6 piece Chicken McNuggets
- 2 medium fries
- 2 small fries
- 2 medium Cokes
- 2 small Cokes

Nutrition facts per person

Calories	900 (average)
Fat	37 grams
Carbohydrates	123 grams
Protein	23 grams

Chicken, Potatoes and Salad for Four
$13.78

A savings of $14.11, or 51%, over the McDonald's meal.

Nutrition facts per person and difference from McDonald's meal

Calories	934	**+4%**
Fat	39 grams	**+5%**
Carbohydrates	80 grams	**−35%**
Protein	67 grams	**+191%**

Prices per item:

Milk $1.49
Bread $.75
Chicken $5.96
Lettuce $1.50
Oil $.55
Potatoes $2.98
Salt and pepper $.05
Lemon $.50

Pinto Beans and Rice for Four
$9.26

A savings of $18.63, or 67%, over the McDonald's meal.

Nutrition facts per person and difference from McDonald's meal

Calories	571	**−37%**
Fat	15 grams	**−59%**
Carbohydrates	83 grams	**−33%**
Protein	26 grams	**+13%**

Prices per item:

Milk $1.49
Bell pepper $3.00
Onion $.37
Beans $2.00
Rice $.50
Salt and pepper $.05

Taken from: Mark Bittman. "Is Junk Food Really Cheaper?" *New York Times*, September 24, 2011.

says Julie Guthman, associate professor of community studies at the University of California, Santa Cruz, and author of the forthcoming *Weighing In: Obesity, Food Justice and the Limits of Capitalism* [published in 2011]. "Their reaction is, 'Let me enjoy what I want to eat, and stop telling me what to do.' And it's one of the few things that less well-off people have: they don't have to cook."

It's not just about choice, however, and rational arguments go only so far, because money and access and time and skill are not the only considerations. The ubiquity, convenience and habit-forming appeal of hyperprocessed foods have largely drowned out the alternatives: there are five fast-food restaurants for every supermarket in the United States; in recent decades the adjusted for inflation price of fresh produce has increased by 40 percent while the price of soda and processed food has decreased by as much as 30 percent; and nearly inconceivable resources go into encouraging consumption in restaurants: fast-food companies spent $4.2 billion on marketing in 2009.

Furthermore, the engineering behind hyperprocessed food makes it virtually addictive. A 2009 study by the Scripps Research Institute indicates that overconsumption of fast food "triggers addiction-like neuroaddictive responses" in the brain, making it harder to trigger the release of dopamine. In other words the more fast food we eat, the more we need to give us pleasure; thus the report suggests that the same mechanisms underlie drug addiction and obesity.

This addiction to processed food is the result of decades of vision and hard work by the industry. For 50 years, says David A. Kessler, former commissioner of the Food and Drug Administration and author of *The End of Overeating*, companies strove to create food that was "energy-dense, highly stimulating, and went down easy. They put it on every street corner and made it mobile, and they made it socially acceptable to eat anytime and anyplace. They created a food carnival, and that's where we live. And if you're used to self-stimulation every 15 minutes, well, you can't run into the kitchen to satisfy that urge."

To Change Obesity, Change Culture

Real cultural changes are needed to turn this around. Somehow, no-nonsense cooking and eating—roasting a chicken, making a grilled cheese sandwich, scrambling an egg, tossing a salad—must become popular again, and valued not just by hipsters in Brooklyn [New York] or locavores [those who eat only locally grown food] in Berkeley [California]. The smart campaign is not to get McDonald's to serve better food but to get people to see cooking as a joy rather than a burden, or at least as part of a normal life.

As with any addictive behavior, this one is most easily countered by educating children about the better way. Children, after all, are born without bad habits. And yet it's adults who must begin to tear down the food carnival.

The question is how? Efforts are everywhere. The People's Grocery in Oakland secures affordable groceries for low-income people. Zoning laws in Los Angeles [California] restrict the number of fast-food restaurants in high-obesity neighborhoods. There's the Healthy Food Financing Initiative, a successful Pennsylvania program to build fresh food outlets in underserved areas, now being expanded nationally. FoodCorps and Cooking Matters teach young people how to farm and cook.

As Malik Yakini, executive director of the Detroit [Michigan] Black Community Food Security Network, says, "We've seen minor successes, but the food movement is still at the infant stage, and we need a massive social shift to convince people to consider healthier options."

How do you change a culture? The answers, not surprisingly, are complex. "Once I look at what I'm eating," says Dr. Kessler, "and realize it's not food, and I ask 'what am I doing here?' that's the start. It's not about whether I think it's good for me, it's about changing how I feel. And we change how people feel by changing the environment."

We Owe It to Ourselves to Change

Obviously, in an atmosphere where any regulation is immediately labeled "nanny statism," changing "the environment" is difficult.

But we've done this before, with tobacco. The 1998 tobacco settlement limited cigarette marketing and forced manufacturers to finance anti-smoking campaigns—a negotiated change that led to an environmental one that in turn led to a cultural one, after which kids said to their parents, "I wish you didn't smoke." Smoking had to be converted from a cool habit into one practiced by pariahs.

A similar victory in the food world is symbolized by the stories parents tell me of their kids booing as they drive by McDonald's.

To make changes like this more widespread we need action both cultural and political. The cultural lies in celebrating real food; raising our children in homes that don't program them for fast-produced, eaten-on-the-run, high-calorie, low-nutrition junk; giving them the gift of appreciating the pleasures of nourishing one another and enjoying that nourishment together.

Political action would mean agitating to limit the marketing of junk; forcing its makers to pay the true costs of production; recognizing that advertising for fast food is not the exercise of free speech but behavior manipulation of addictive substances; and making certain that real food is affordable and available to everyone. The political challenge is the more difficult one, but it cannot be ignored.

What's easier is to cook at every opportunity, to demonstrate to family and neighbors that the real way is the better way. And even the more fun way: kind of like a carnival.

What You Should Know About Obesity

Obesity in the United States

According to the National Center for Health Statistics, part of the Centers for Disease Control and Prevention, in 2011:

- more than one-third of US adults (35.7 percent) were obese;
- almost 17 percent of youth were obese;
- the prevalence of obesity among adults or children from 2007–2008 to 2009–2010 was unchanged;
- obesity prevalence does not differ between men and women;
- adults aged sixty and over are more likely to be obese than younger adults;
- in 2008 medical costs associated with obesity were estimated at $147 billion;
- medical costs for obese people were $1,429 higher than for those of normal weight;
- non-Hispanic blacks have the highest age-adjusted rates of obesity (49.5 percent), compared with Mexican Americans (40.4 percent), all Hispanics (39.1 percent), and non-Hispanic whites (34.3 percent);
- the South has the highest prevalence of obesity, with 29.5 percent of the population classified as obese;
- the Midwest has the second highest prevalence of obesity, with 29.0 percent of the population classified as obese;
- the Northeast has the third highest prevalence of obesity, with 25.3 percent of the population classified as obese;
- the West has the lowest prevalence of obesity, with 24.3 percent of the population classified as obese;

- Colorado had the lowest obesity prevalence, with 20.7 percent of the population classified as obese;
- Mississippi had the highest obesity prevalence, with 34.9 percent of the population classified as obese;
- no state had a prevalence of obesity less than 20 percent;
- thirty-nine states had a prevalence of 25 percent or more; and
- twelve states had a prevalence of 30 percent or more.

Obesity prevalence by state in 2011 was as follows:

Alabama	32.0	Montana	24.6
Alaska	27.4	Nebraska	28.4
Arizona	24.7	Nevada	24.5
Arkansas	30.9	New Hampshire	26.2
California	23.8	New Jersey	23.7
Colorado	20.7	New Mexico	26.3
Delaware	28.8	New York	24.5
District of Columbia	23.7	North Carolina	29.1
Florida	26.6	North Dakota	27.8
Georgia	28	Ohio	29.6
Hawaii	21.8	Oklahoma	31.1
Idaho	27.0	Oregon	26.7
Illinois	27.1	Pennsylvania	28.6
Indiana	30.8	Rhode Island	25.4
Iowa	29.0	South Carolina	30.8
Kansas	29.6	South Dakota	28.1
Kentucky	30.4	Tennessee	29.2
Louisiana	33.4	Texas	30.4
Maine	27.8	Utah	24.4
Maryland	28.3	Vermont	25.4
Massachusetts	22.7	Virginia	29.2
Michigan	31.3	Washington	26.5
Minnesota	25.7	West Virginia	32.4
Mississippi	34.9	Wisconsin	27.7
Missouri	30.3	Wyoming	25.0

American Opinions on Obesity

A 2012 *Washington Post*/Kaiser Family Foundation poll asked Americans whether they support or oppose putting a special tax on junk foods such as soda, chips, and candy, and using the money for programs to fight obesity:

- Fifty-three percent supported such a program.
- Forty-seven percent opposed it.
- One percent were unsure.

A 2012 Gallup poll found that obesity outranks other health issues about which Americans are concerned. When asked how serious they thought the problem of cigarettes, alcohol, and obesity are:

- 38 percent said obesity is an extremely serious problem;
- 43 percent said it is a very serious problem;
- 15 percent said it is a somewhat serious problem;
- 3 percent said it is not a problem;
- 1 percent were unsure;

- 30 percent said cigarettes are an extremely serious problem;
- 37 percent said they are a very serious problem;
- 27 percent said they are a somewhat serious problem;
- 6 percent said they are not a problem;
- 1 percent were unsure;

- 18 percent said alcohol is an extremely serious problem;
- 28 percent said it is a very serious problem;
- 38 percent said it is a somewhat serious problem;
- 12 percent said it is not a problem;
- 2 percent were unsure.

Taken together,

- 81 percent of Americans think obesity is an extremely or very serious problem;
- 67 percent of Americans think smoking is an extremely or very serious problem; and
- 47 percent think alcohol is an extremely or very serious problem.

The poll also asked Americans how important they think it is to have federal government programs that address health risks associated with each of the three issues, and

- 23 percent said it is extremely important to have such programs for obesity;
- 34 percent said it is very important to have such programs for obesity;
- 22 percent said it is somewhat important to have such programs for obesity;
- 19 percent said it is not important to have such programs for obesity;
- 2 percent were unsure;

- 21 percent said it is extremely important to have such programs for smoking;
- 34 percent said it is very important to have such programs for smoking;
- 25 percent said it is somewhat important to have such programs for smoking;
- 19 percent said it is not important to have such programs for smoking;
- 2 percent were unsure;

- 18 percent said it is extremely important to have such programs for excessive consumption of alcohol;
- 30 percent said it is very important to have such programs for excessive consumption of alcohol;
- 30 percent said it is somewhat important to have such programs for excessive consumption of alcohol;
- 20 percent said it is not important to have such programs for excessive consumption of alcohol; and
- 2 percent were unsure.

The level at which government should be involved in solving the obesity problem differed among political parties:

- Seventy-nine percent of Republicans said obesity is an extremely or very serious problem, but only 27 percent thought it was extremely or very important for the government to have programs that address it.

- Eighty-one percent of Independents said obesity is an extremely or very serious problem, while 55 percent thought it was extremely or very important for the government to have programs that address it.

- Eighty-three percent of Democrats said obesity is an extremely or very serious problem, while 82 percent thought it was extremely or very important for the government to have programs that address it.

A 2012 Rasmussen Reports poll found that

- 82 percent of Americans think childhood obesity is a serious problem in the United States;
- 13 percent do not think it is a serious issue; and
- 5 percent were unsure.

What You Should Do About Obesity

As you have learned from this book, there are numerous reasons why people become overweight or obese. Sometimes, these reasons are socioeconomic—people who live in neighborhoods where fresh, healthy food is scarce, or too expensive, may struggle with obesity more than those who live in neighborhoods where fresh, healthy food is abundant. People who have more income are also more likely to buy healthier, fresher, more expensive foods than cheaper, fattier, saltier ones, although it can be inexpensive to eat healthy.

Sometimes obesity stems from personal or emotional issues. Food is abundant in American society—much of it tastes good and is convenient. We often turn to food to cope with stress, depression, or to otherwise soothe ourselves. We also tend to celebrate via food (try to think of a holiday, event, or party that did not involve food of some sort) and many of us live in communities or climates in which getting regular exercise takes more effort and time than some are willing to invest.

For most people, barring a health disorder or unique condition, losing weight typically involves the tried-and-true combination of eating healthy and less and getting more exercise. There are no shortcuts, tricks, or secrets to losing weight, and programs that claim to offer these are usually selling something. Although losing weight takes a fair amount of discipline and hard work, it almost always pays off if you follow certain steps and put your mind to it.

Eating Better

To eat better, let members of your family know you would like to eat more fruits and vegetables, lean proteins (like chicken breast, egg whites, tofu, or turkey slices), whole grains (such as brown rice, quinoa, whole-grain breads and pastas), and cut back on high-calorie sauces, cheeses, fats, and processed and junk foods. Ask your family to support you by preparing meals that feature these foods. If they do not know how to cook them, learn together—numerous websites and videos offer healthy, quick, and affordable recipe ideas, with plenty of instructional support. Also ask if you can accompany your parent or guardian on a trip to the grocery store so you can participate in the process of picking out healthy snacks and meal ingredients. An often-overlooked key to eating well is preparing in advance to do so. Keep healthy snacks (like sliced veggies and hummus, fresh fruit, cheese sticks, and salads) on hand, ready to go for when you get hungry. Take the time to pack a lunch so you are not forced to grab something quickly or buy something unhealthy. Do not skip meals—this interferes with your metabolism and can lead to your actually putting on weight.

A good idea while trying to eat better is to keep a food journal of everything you eat in a given day. Food journals are important because they make us aware of the mindless snacking we do that tends to result in weight gain. When we eat a complete meal at an established mealtime, we often remember what we ate and how much. But we can consume a lot of calories when we are not even paying attention—some people eat an additional five hundred calories or more per day through snacking or "invisible" eating, such as taking tastes of food while they cook, digging into a candy dish on someone's desk, or sharing a few chips from a friend's bag.

Keeping a food journal, therefore, may make you aware of everything you eat. You may think you just had some scrambled eggs, a turkey sandwich, and a bowl of macaroni and cheese in the course of one day; keeping a food journal may reveal that you also ate two granola bars, a handful of peanuts, three cookies, a few bites of ice cream, and drank a cup of hot chocolate. Before you can eat better, you must become aware of what you are actually eating.

Measuring the amount of food you consume is also important. It is hard to get a sense of what exactly constitutes a portion if you eat pretzels out of the bag or peanut butter right out of the jar. Make an effort to measure all of your foods. This not only helps you take stock of what you are eating but also gives you a sense of what it takes to fill you up. Starting with one cup of pretzels, rather than the whole bag, may encourage you to wait and see if you feel full before you finish the entire bag.

There are certain activities and situations that make us more prone to mindless eating, and more vulnerable to eating unhealthy foods. Avoid eating while watching television, for example—it is too easy to space out and keep putting food in your mouth without actually checking to see whether your stomach wants it. Likewise, avoid eating when you are bored or unsure what to do with yourself. Start to become aware of what situations make you prone to junk snacking or poor eating, and find ways to avoid or minimize them.

Moving Around More

As important as one's diet is the amount and type of exercise one gets. If you are overweight or obese, exercise is probably uncomfortable for you. It does not feel good, or you fear you lack skill; perhaps you feel embarrassed while doing it. Know that exercising is always hardest in the beginning. Jogging even one block when you are out of shape can feel like running a marathon. Few people like doing things they feel bad at from the start or embarking on activities that feel overwhelmingly challenging.

Like other challenges, exercise is something you can improve at, provided you take it one step at a time. There are many "couch to 5K" programs that help even the most inexperienced people train to run more than 3 miles (5km) by taking the process one step at a time. Using various motivational tools and applications, they encourage you to start out slowly by alternating walking and running, to not think about the goal right at first, and to just concentrate on learning to increase your tolerance and conditioning one step at a time. By the time you are ready to go a little farther, a little faster, your body will be able to do so.

The federal government recommends that kids and teens between six and seventeen years of age get at least sixty minutes of physical activity per day, five days a week, for six out of eight weeks. Or, you can make sure you do a lot of walking: The government recommends that girls walk at least eleven thousand steps per day, while boys should walk at least thirteen thousand steps per day. Help yourself walk more by walking to school, taking the stairs instead of an escalator or elevator, taking the long way around a building, or parking farther away from the store or other destination; in bad weather, you can walk around a mall or other indoor area.

As you strive to eat healthy and get an appropriate amount of exercise, remember to never lose sight of what your goals are. Why do you want to change your eating and exercise habits? Is it to look a certain way? Is it to feel better? Is it to avoid health problems? Always eat healthy and exercise for *yourself* and not for someone else. Also, losing more than a half to one pound per week can be equally unhealthy, so be sure to take your weight loss slowly, reasonably, and healthfully.

The editors have compiled the following list of organizations concerned with the issues debated in this book. The descriptions are derived from materials provided by the organizations. All have publications or information available for interested readers. The list was compiled on the date of publication of the present volume; names, addresses, phone and fax numbers, and e-mail and Internet addresses may change. Be aware that many organizations take several weeks or longer to respond to inquiries, so allow as much time as possible.

American Diabetes Association (ADA)
1701 N. Beauregard St.
Alexandria, VA 22311
(800) 342-2383
e-mail: askada@diabetes.org
website: www.diabetes.org

Diabetes is often an obesity-related disease that the ADA, a not-for-profit health advocacy organization, works to prevent and cure. Since food and good nutrition are critical to managing diabetes, the ADA educates people about changing their lifestyle and about disease prevention. As a part of its program, the ADA provides a guide to eating out and tips for how to order more healthful items while dining at restaurants and fast-food establishments.

American Obesity Association (AOA)
8757 Georgia Ave., Ste. 1320
Silver Spring, MD 20910
(301) 563-6526
website: www.obesity.org

The AOA is the leading scientific organization dedicated to the study of obesity and its health effects. Its researchers seek to understand the causes and treatment of obesity while also keeping the medical community informed of the latest advances in research. It publishes the journal *Obesity*, and several newsletters and reports found on its website discuss what causes obesity and how it can be reduced and prevented.

Center for Science in the Public Interest (CSPI)
1220 L St. NW, Ste. 300
Washington, DC 20005
(202) 332-9110
website: www.cspinet.org

Formed in 1971, CSPI is a nonprofit education and consumer advocacy organization dedicated to fighting for government food policies and corporate practices that promote healthy diets. CSPI also works to prevent deceptive marketing practices and ensures that science is used for public welfare. It publishes *Nutrition Action Healthletter*, the most widely circulated health newsletter in North America. CSPI seeks to educate the public, advocate for government policies that are consistent with scientific evidence on health and environmental issues, and counter industry's powerful influence on public opinion and public policies. CSPI supports food labeling and government efforts aimed at reducing the amount of sugar, salt, and fat Americans eat.

Centers for Disease Control and Prevention (CDC)
Division of Nutrition and Physical Activity (DNPA)
1600 Clifton Rd.
Atlanta, GA 30333
(800) CDC-INFO (232-4636)
e-mail: cdcinfo@cdc.gov
website: www.cdc.gov/nccdphp/dnpa/

The CDC is part of the US Department of Health and Human Services (DHHS). Its Division of Nutrition and Physical Activity has three focus areas: nutrition, physical activity, and overweight and obesity. The DNPA addresses the role of nutrition and physical activity in improving the public's health. DNPA activities include health promotion, research, training, and education. The DNPA maintains an overweight and obesity website on which it provides many helpful charts, maps, and reports related to overweight and obesity.

Food Marketing Institute (FMI)
2345 Crystal Dr., Ste. 800
Arlington, VA 22202
(202) 452.8444
website: www.fmi.org

FMI conducts programs in public affairs, food safety, research and education, and industry relations on behalf of food retailers and wholesalers in the United States and around the globe. By pursuing these activities, FMI provides leadership and advocacy for the food distribution industry as it innovates to meet customers' changing needs. The Health and Wellness section on its website provides information about nutrition, nutrition labeling, and obesity.

Food Research and Action Center (FRAC)
1875 Connecticut Ave. NW, Ste. 540
Washington, DC 20009
(202) 986-2200
website: www.frac.org

FRAC is the leading national nonprofit organization working to improve public policies and public-private partnerships to eradicate hunger and undernutrition in the United States. FRAC has published many papers about the link between hunger and obesity and works with hundreds of national, state, and local nonprofit organizations, public agencies, and corporations to address this and other food-related problems that plague Americans.

International Association for the Study of Obesity (IASO)
Charles Darwin House
12 Roger St.
London WC1N 2JU
United Kingdom
e-mail: enquiries@iaso.org
website: www.iaso.org

The IASO is a nongovernmental organization with forty-nine member associations representing fifty-three countries. Its mission is to improve global health by promoting the understanding of obesity and weight-related diseases through scientific research and discussion. The IASO works with the UN's World Health Organization and other global nongovernmental organizations toward this goal.

Mission: Readiness
1212 New York Ave. NW, Ste. 300
Washington, DC 20005
(202) 464-5224
e-mail: mjayne@missionreadiness.org
website: www.missionreadiness.org

This is a nonpartisan national security organization composed of senior retired military leaders. Their mission is to call for smart investments in America's children so that America's future military candidates are able and ready. According to Mission: Readiness, 75 percent of seventeen- to twenty-four-year-olds in the United States cannot serve in the military, primarily because they are physically unfit, have not graduated from high school, or have a criminal record. A key part of the organization's goal is to reduce child obesity rates so more young people may be qualified for service.

Obesity Action Coalition (OAC)
4511 N. Himes Ave., Ste. 250
Tampa, FL33614
(800) 717-3117
e-mail: info@obesityaction.org
website: www.obesityaction.org

The OAC educates obesity patients, their families, and the public. It provides links to resources and obesity support groups throughout the United States. The OAC works against the negative stigma of obesity and is an advocate for safe and effective obesity treatment.

Obesity in America
8401 Connecticut Ave., Ste. 900
Chevy Chase, MD 20815
(301) 941-0200
website: www.obesityinamerica.org

A creation of the Endocrine Society and the Hormone Health Network, Obesity in America serves as a one-stop clearinghouse for those who seek information on the scientific trends and advancements that may one day lead to a slimmer, fitter America. The organization publishes numerous reports on America's obesity problem, and students will find many useful statistics, charts, and maps at its website.

The Obesity Society
8630 Fenton St., Ste. 814
Silver Spring, MD 20910
(301) 563-6526
website: www.obesity.org

The Obesity Society is the leading scientific society dedicated to the study of obesity. Since 1982 the Obesity Society has been committed to encouraging research on the causes and treatment of obesity and to keeping the medical community and public informed of new advances.

Overeaters Anonymous (OA)
PO Box 44020
Rio Rancho, NM 87174-4020
(505) 891-2664
e-mail: info@oa.org
website: www.oa.org

OA is open to individuals who wish to or are recovering from compulsive overeating. Individuals share their experiences and support each other to stop eating compulsively. OA provides a 12-step program, modeled after that of Alcoholics Anonymous, to help members control their food addictions. Members can attend face-to-face meetings in their own localities and can communicate with members worldwide via the Internet.

Rudd Center for Food Policy & Obesity
Yale University
309 Edwards St.
New Haven, CT 06511
website: www.yaleruddcenter.org

A nonprofit research and public policy organization devoted to improving the world's diet, preventing obesity, and reducing weight stigma, the center serves as a leading research institution and clearinghouse for resources that add to the understanding of the complex forces affecting how we eat, how we stigmatize overweight and obese people, and how we can change.

US Department of Agriculture (USDA)
Food and Nutrition Service (FNS)
1400 Independence Ave. SW
Washington, DC 20250
(202) 720-2791
website: www.usda.gov

The FNS is an agency of the USDA that is responsible for administering the nation's domestic nutrition assistance programs. It provides prepared meals, food assistance, and nutrition education materials to one in five Americans. The agency also encourages children and teens to follow the healthy eating guidelines set by MyPyramid in its "Eat Smart, Play Hard" campaign.

Weight-Control Information Network (WIN)
1 WIN Way
Bethesda, MD 20892-3665
e-mail: win@info.niddk.nih.gov
website: http://win.niddk.nih.gov

WIN is an information service of the National Institute of Diabetes and Digestive and Kidney Diseases (NIDDK). It provides science-based and up-to-date information on weight control, obesity, physical activity, and related nutritional issues.

BIBLIOGRAPHY

Books

Eric A. Finkelstein and Laurie Zuckerman, *The Fattening of America: How The Economy Makes Us Fat, if It Matters, and What to Do About It*. Hoboken, NJ: Wiley, 2008.

Julie Guthman, *Weighing In: Obesity, Food Justice, and the Limits of Capitalism*. Berkeley: University of California Press, 2011.

Zoe Harcombe, *The Obesity Epidemic: What Caused It? How Can We Stop It?* London: Columbus, 2010.

John Luik, Patrick Basham, and Gio Gori, *Diet Nation: Exposing the Obesity Crusade*. London: Social Affairs Unit, 2006.

Marion Nestle and Malden Nesheim, *Why Calories Count: From Science to Politics*. Berkeley: University of California Press, 2012.

J. Eric Oliver, *Fat Politics: The Real Story Behind America's Obesity Epidemic*. New York: Oxford University Press, 2005.

Michael Pollan and Maira Kalman, *Food Rules: An Eater's Manual*. London: Penguin, 2011.

Gary Taubes, *Why We Get Fat: And What to Do About It*. New York: Anchor, 2010.

Karl Weber, ed., *Food Inc.: A Participant Guide; How Industrial Food Is Making Us Sicker, Fatter, and Poorer—and What You Can Do About It*. New York: PublicAffairs, 2009.

Periodicals and Internet Sources

Jeffrey Algazy, Steven Gipstein, Farhad Riahi, and Katherine Tryon, "Why Governments Must Lead the Fight Against Obesity," *McKinsey Quarterly*, October 2010.

James A. Bacon, "Link Between Poverty and Obesity," *Washington Times*, November 18, 2011.

Frank Bruni, ". . . and Love Handles for All," *New York Times*, April 16, 2012.

Trevor Butterworth, "The Class War on Fat," Daily, August 1, 2011. www.thedaily.com/page/2011/08/01/080111-opinions -column-class-butterworth-1-2/.

Art Carden, "Taxing Sugar Will Do More Harm than Good," *U.S. News and World Report*, March 30, 2012.

Center for Consumer Freedom, "Big Fat Lies," 2012. www.consum erfreedom.com/issues/big-fat-lies/.

Roberta Clark, "What's the Return on Fighting Obesity?," *Boston Globe*, September 24, 2009.

Christopher C. Cook, "The Food Divide," *San Francisco Bay Guardian*, November 29, 2011.

Fergus Cullen, "Government Shouldn't Take Choice Off the Table," *Hartford (CT) Courant*, July 11, 2010.

Brent Cunningham and Jane Black, "The New Front in the Culture Wars: Food," *Washington Post*, November 26, 2010.

Michael Davidson, Donald Storm, and D. Allen Youngman, "Childhood Obesity Threat to National Security," *Lexington (KY) Herald Leader*, June 27, 2011.

Joanna Dolgoff, "Should Child Obesity Be Considered Child Abuse?," *Huffington Post*, April 13, 2010. www.huffingtonpost .com/joanna-dolgoff-md/should-child-obesity-be-c_b_508680 .html.

Daniel Engber, "Does Poverty Make People Obese, or Is It the Other Way Around?," *Slate*, September 28, 2009. www.slate .com/articles/health_and_science/science/2009/09/give_me _your_tired_your_poor_your_big_fat_asses_.single.html.

Christy M. Glass, Steven A. Haas, and Eric N. Reither, "Heavy in School, Burdened for Life," *New York Times*, June 2, 2011.

Dan Glickman, Ann M. Veneman, Donna E. Shalala, and Mike Leavitt, "Lots to Lose—How Obesity Is Costing America," *Hill*, June 4, 2012. http://thehill.com/opinion/op-ed/230831-lots-to -lose-how-obesity-is-costing-america-.

David Gratzer, "The McVictim Syndrome Could Kill Us," *Los Angeles Times*, December 8, 2010.

Julie Gunlock, "Anti-obesity Efforts Are Fattening Government," Townhall, June 12, 2012. http://townhall.com/columnists/juliegunlock/2012/06/12/antiobesity_efforts_are_fattening_government.

Arvene Kilby, "Government's Not Cause nor Cure in Obesity Spike," NJ.com, May 20, 2012. www.nj.com/gloucester/voices/index.ssf/2012/05/governments_not_cause_nor_cure.html.

Lucy Komisar, "School Lunches and the Food Industry," *New York Times*, December 3, 2011.

Robert H. Lustig, Laura A. Schmidt, and Claire D. Brindis, "The Toxic Truth About Sugar," *Nature*, February 2, 2012.

Rob Lyons, "The Onward March of the Obesity Orwellians," Spiked, September 7, 2011. www.spiked-online.com/site/article/11056/.

Katherine Mangu-War, "McDonald's to Kids: Apple Slices for All, Whether or Not You Want Them," *Reason*, July 26, 2011.

Lindsey Murtagh and David S. Ludwig, "State Intervention in Life-Threatening Childhood Obesity," *Journal of the American Medical Association*, July 13, 2011.

Ruben Navarette, "Taking Obese Child from Mom Is Wrong," CNN.com, December 2, 2011. www.cnn.com/2011/12/02/opinion/navarrette-obese-child/index.html.

Jessica Pauline Ogilvie, "Should Morbidly Obese Children Be Taken from Parents?," *Los Angeles Times*, August 29, 2011.

Kathleen Parker, "Health Reform and Obesity: Eat, Drink, and Watch Out," *Washington Post*, May 20, 2011.

———, "They Ate Cake, and Then Had a Bag of Chips," *Chicago Tribune*, May 10, 2012.

Tara Parker-Pope, "The Fat Trap," *New York Times*, December 28, 2011.

Tomas J. Philipson and Richard A. Posner, "Fat New World," *Wall Street Journal*, July 31, 2010.

Alice Randall, "Black Women and Fat," *New York Times*, May 6, 2012.

Laura Schmidt, "Why We Should Regulate Sugar Like Alcohol," CNN.com, February 1, 2012. www.cnn.com/2012/02/01/health /opinion-regulate-sugar-alcohol/index.html.

John M. Shalikashvili and Hugh Shelton, "The Latest National Security Threat: Obesity," *Washington Post*, April 30, 2010.

Jeff Stier and David W. Almasi, "Obesity Forecast Is Overblown," *Newsday*, May 9, 2012.

Gary Taubes, "What Really Makes Us Fat," *New York Times*, June 30, 2012.

Helen Zoe Veit, "Time to Revive Home Ec," *New York Times*, September 5, 2011.

Joanna Weiss, "Striking a Nerve on Childhood Obesity," *Boston Globe*, July 24, 2011.

Zoe Williams, "Obesity Is About Poverty and Cheap Food, Not a Lack of Moral Fibre," *Guardian* (Manchester, UK), December 14, 2011.

Websites

Americans Against Food Taxes (www.nofoodtaxes.com). This site represents a coalition of various entities that range from individuals to large corporations. Together, they oppose taxes on food that are designed to punish certain eating behaviors.

Calculate Your BMI (www.nhlbisupport.com/bmi/). This site, run by the National Heart, Lung, and Blood Institute, lets users calculate their body mass index (BMI) by inputting their height and weight.

Centers for Disease Control and Prevention, Obesity Page (www.cdc.gov/obesity/). This government site offers numerous statistics, maps, and charts about obesity and overweight in the United States. It can be very helpful for students looking for supportive material for presentations or reports.

Food Politics (www.foodpolitics.com). This website was born out of Marion Nestle's work on the politics of food, health, and obesity. It frequently links to breaking news or study results that have an impact on these topics.

Jamie Oliver's Food Revolution (www.jamieoliver.com/us/foun dation/jamies-food-revolution/home). Celebrity chef Jamie Oliver has made it his mission to eradicate obesity and introduce healthy eating to America's homes and schools. This website documents his efforts and successes.

Kids' Safe & Healthful Foods Project (www.healthyschoolfood snow.org). This site, run jointly by the Pew Charitable Trusts and the Robert Wood Johnson Foundation, contains news and updates about developments in school lunch policies.

Let's Move! (www.letsmove.gov/). This health program launched by First Lady Michelle Obama aims to wipe out childhood obesity within a generation. The program's website contains lots of useful tips for getting exercise, eating healthy, and growing your own food.

The Lunch Tray (www.thelunchtray.com). This site provides good commentary on articles, op-eds, news releases, and other pieces of media regarding children and food both in school and out.

Robert Wood Johnson Foundation's Child Obesity Page (www .rwjf.org/en/about-rwjf/program-areas/childhood-obesity.html). This page offers a plethora of authoritative information about topics relating to child obesity, such as its prevalence and programs to reduce it.

Tray Talk (www.traytalk.org). This site, sponsored by the School Nutrition Association, offers news updates on topics related to healthy eating, food in schools, and child obesity. It offers recipes, success stories, and other useful information.

Coronary heart disease (CHD), 10–11, 12
Courtemanche, Charles J., 47

D
Danesh, John, 16
Department of Agriculture, US (USDA), 72, 77, 82
Diabetes, type 2, 12
Draper, Alexander, 57

E
Education level, prevalence of obesity by, 39
The End of Overeating (Kessler), 91
Environmental Working Group, 78

F
Fast foods. See Junk foods/soda
Fat cells, 33
Field, Penny, 27, 28, 29
Flegal, Katherine, 19
Food deserts, 88
Food industry
  is not responsible for obesity epidemic, 30–31
  opposition to junk food tax by, 62
  opposition to updating USDA guidelines on school lunches by, 72–73
  spending on marketing by, 91
Food Research and Action Center, 46
Foods. See Healthy foods; Junk foods

Freedman, Dan, 5–6
Freedman, David H., 6, 8

G
Gallstones, 14
Gastric bypass surgery, 11
Genetics, linked between obesity and, 35, 36
Goldstein, Harold, 65, 66
Government
  role in dietary control is problematic, 68–70
  role in reducing childhood obesity, 73
  should not play role in curbing obesity, 28–31
  suggested actions to reduce childhood obesity by, 26, 73
Gray, Jerri, 56, 57
Guthman, Julie, 89, 91
GymPact, 8

H
Health risks, of obesity, 10–14
  in children, 14
  costs associated with, 25–26, 38, 46
  have been exaggerated, 15–20
Healthy foods, 74, 77, 83
  amount one dollar buys of, 84
  are cheap enough/American do not choose them, 86–93
  people with higher socioeconomic status consume more, 39–40
  subsidizing of, can reduce obesity, 81–85